Fourth Printing of Edition 3.0.8 (2008)

Printed in the United States of America

Library of Congress Catalog Second Edition is 95-92913

ISBN 978-0-9638793-7-0 Paper

also available as e-book edition ISBN 978-0-9638793-9-4

www.paperclayart.com

New Century Arts Inc.
PO Box 9060
Seattle, WA 98109 USA

PaperCLAY

For Ceramic Sculptors **A Studio Companion**

Edition 3.0.8 by **Rosette Gault**

Contents

Dedication

to artists
and all people
who supply fresh works of
wonder, imagination, beauty, and vision
to mankind.

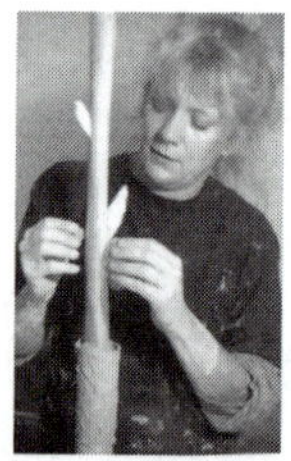

***Within** this book find answers to hundreds of practical questions about ceramic paper clay as a medium.*

See what high performance ceramic paperclay can "do" that would be impossible with a traditional clay.

Although the finished fired result in earthenware, terra cotta, raku, stoneware, or porcelain may feel and look the same as if it was made of traditional clay, there are some special "rules" and differences about it.

Chapter One offers a quick review of the beginner basic hand skills for clay work from the view of paperclay.

Chapter Two, on page 17, answers questions from intermediate and advanced level artists for projects such as: figurative or abstract sculpture by addition and/or subtraction, carving, chiseling, modeling, bas relief, tile, and wall work. High, mid, low, and "non" fire sculpture ideas are shown.

Chapter Three, on page 35, explains success tips specific to the stages and timing involved to build large scale sculpture. Big plaster molds and sand cast methods are shown as well the adjustments to balance in the recipe for large work.

Adaptations for pottery are discussed on Chapter Four on page 71.

Chapter Five guides artists who prepare paper clay batches in studio "from scratch" with recycled papers and pulps made from them.

At the end of the book is a resource area with more technical help regarding firing, finish, further study and research areas.

A detailed index is included.

Quick View

What is paper clay?

Ceramic paperclay contains a special balance of cellulose fibers (like those in paper pulp) dispersed uniformly within a base of traditional clay. Types include: low-fire white earthenware, red terra cotta, majolica, china clay, raku, porcelain, stoneware, salt, and combinations of these clays. In other words, most clay can be transformed into a paperclay version. It is possible to make paper pulp and economically in your studio with simple tools. Paper clay has strong green strength. When fired, it can be lighter weight than traditional clay. Paperclay serves the imagination of artists and designers like no other medium can. Let this book be a bridge from your imagination to ceramic form.

Whats so special about it?

With traditional clay works must be successfully assembled at the leatherhard state before the clay dries out and this was a technical limit. In comparison, with a properly balanced paperclay the artist has freedom to or assemble, join, repair, cut, model over at the bone dry and even sometimes the fired state. Traditional clay at the bone dry state before firing is far more vulnerable than a paperclay is.

Can ceramic paperclay be worked in the hands like a traditional clay, ie. wedge, coil, slab, model and wheel?

Yes. More choice is available to you than with traditional clay however. For example, arrange fresh coils without always having the step of scoring between them or having to keep them leatherhard to work on. Let the shapes harden to bone dry. It's easy then, to wipe a layer of wet paperclay slurry for instant seal in any gaps. Those who try it find it is both similar and different to tradition.

Are paper clay sculptures easier to transport to the kiln?

Yes, paper fibers can nearly double the green strength before fire. If "anything happens" while en-route to the kiln, a repair to bone state paperclay is usually possible. If the work had been made of traditional clay, repair at bone dry state fails.

Can I fire paper clay in the kiln with ceramic glaze finish?

Yes, provided there is more clay in the clay body than there is cellulose paper fiber. The clay part survives the heat of flame and fire intact. The paper fibers inside the clay evaporate in burnout during at the first hours of the heating period.

I don't have a kiln. I just want to play and try a little. Can I do an air set finish?

Yes. Some decorative forms really don't need to be fired. Plus, a few air dried forms of paperclay are more easy to handle and less brittle bone dried than they will be they are fired.

What new forms in ceramic can now be realized with simple and economical paper clay?

This question can only be answered by an artist whose imagination would be well served with such a medium in his or her hands.

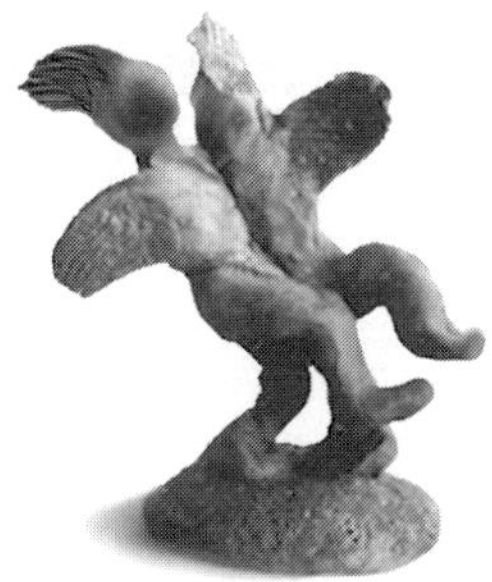

Toward Perspective

It was 1958 or so. At the grand old age of seven, I mused. "Clay? Feels pretty good. I like it." With glee, I joined some wet and dry shapes. Alas, it was only a matter of time before I was in trouble. The brittle dried clay fell apart in my little hands and the answer was: "So very sorry, dear. You'll just have to make another!"

'Re-do the work? That's no fun! Something is definitely NOT OK about this.' I wondered. Why did I question it? Surely I was not the only child who suspected a similar but different form of modeling clay existed. But where?

Nearly 20 years ago, in the mind set for traditional clay, I knew from experience that there was no healing possible at the bone dried state. In despair, frustration, and rebellion, I patched the big stress crack in a large dried out paperclay sculpture with fresh slurry in spite of the rule. Imagine my surprise when, the wound dried and sealed with no scar. Something UNUSUAL HAD HAPPENED with my paperclay mixture, but what? That day, I had "found" the "right balance" between paper pulp and clay. Could I trust it? I kept the risky but wonderful result to myself while I tested to find the firing limits. Soon, I was relying on my recipes of paperclay for my art. The next step was to gently invite artists to wing it with me. So I shared what I knew, artist to artist, and heart to heart. Let's play leapfrog, explore, and enjoy this medium sooner rather than later. Thankfully, artists claimed the aspects of it that served their imagination, and taught what they understood forward.

A field of study has evolved. Perhaps, scientists and engineers may already see potential application involving ceramic paperclays from this. For those who would undertake the appropriate research, some possible directions on the horizon are mentioned in this revision updated to Feb. 2008.

Rosette Gault

Chapter one

Beginner and Classroom Try-Outs

1

Review the Basics

If you have prior experience with traditional clay, the review of the basics here will give you a hands-on feel for how different yet similar paperclay is to handle than a traditional clay you may be used to. Try to make paperclay "do" what the traditional clay could never do. Put it to the test.

If you are new to hand modeling, welcome to a birthright pleasure in life. Anyone who ever wanted to learn, even the so called "talented ones" was a beginner with some patience and a sense of humor. Clear off a table, get a pencil, a hand towel, little sponge and improvise as you go along and get the knack of it. If some of the terms are new to you see page 18, or a glossary. Reading about this is not the same as the feel and touch of it.

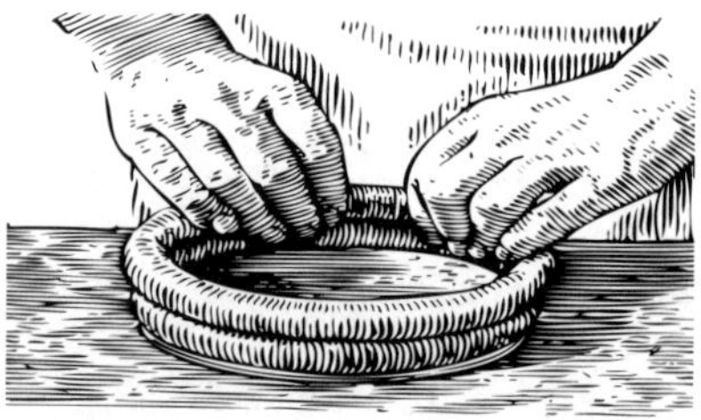

Get a sense of the timing of the work sessions. Paperclay changes from soft to solid over time as it dries out. Unlike traditional clay, the state of bone dry continues to be an active and useful time in the process. You gain the freedom to switch between dry hard and soft state paperclay to your heart's desire before the finish. Understand what can or can't be done to paperclay at each of its various moisture states.

Have a chance to "practice" durable joins that tend to stick better to each other at the bone dried stage than they would at leather hard stage.

Since it's so easy to exchange, attach or replace most parts like handles, ears, tails, and so forth, when the whole piece is at the bone dried stage, plan for this. Work sometimes over dry, on purpose. There's no hurry to complete at leatherhard state like in the past. Nor is there need to cover or baby the projects between work periods like in traditional clay. Attach and remove different styles of handle before you commit to the one you truly like best. Focus can be more on ideas and imagination, and less on the cautions.

To conclude the work session, coat with a sealer of gloss glaze that melts smooth in a single kiln firing. As an alternative, airset finishes will work too.

Coil Practice

Roll out a soft coil with palms of hands on a smooth tabletop, not over newspaper. Vary your palm pressure and notice how the paper clay responds, picks up texture, and etc. Get a sense of how to your "touch" and see its effect on the paperclay. Get a sense of when the clay gets too stiff, dry, or overworked. Place new coils end to end, start a long spiral around, and up. Or, balance a stack of soft coil rings upon one another. Tack the coils in position gently with your fingers. Find a rhythm of gentle repetition of hand motions to help.

If the coil were traditional clay you would have to score or scratch and add some slurry between each coil of paperclay and in order finish before the clay dried out. With paperclay, sealing gaps between the coils can happen **after** the coils are dry.

If new shapes are too floppy, rest them on the side. The can even be force dried near a heat source, or in the sun. Stand them up and or connect them back into your project in the next work period.

Minimize use of water on wet or leatherhard state paperclay. But use generously over bone dried. Try wiping bone dried state of paperclay with a damp sponge of water, the moisture will soak in to paperclay but it will take a while deform the dried coils. Bone dry is my preferred time to apply a coating of P'Slip (watered down P'Clay in a cup) by brush or small damp sponge and quickly fill in between coil openings or repair unintended cracks. Rub down the surface of the coils to trim and neaten up the piece. Try also braids, twists, ribbons

Seal Between Coils After They Dry: *To start, use softer P'Clay before it stiffens too much. Set coils gently in any position. Let them go dry in the air, near heaters, or even direct sun. Shown to right is a spiral that sits in an open bowl. Next day, or so, lift out the perfectly hard dry bowl. To seal between openings, simply paint a thin layer of P'Slip over them. To trim before firing, rub with a damp sponge until satisfied. For a "footed" bowl, maybe finish with a new coil ring underneath.*

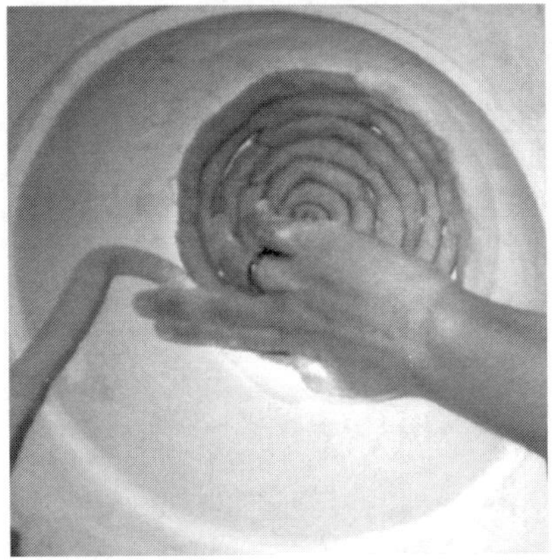

(flattened coils), interweaving, baskets, curli-Qs, as skill improves.

If you wanted to cover up seam lines at bone dry, apply a layer of very soft P'Clay or super thick P'Slip. Bone dry coils will keep their shape even when they are re-soaked and re-wetted by watery sponges multiple times on multiple work periods. Sometimes I dip all or part of the bone dry coil in the P'slip before I attach it to another dry one. Work in the bone dried state stores easily and indefinitely. No plastic wrapping is needed.

Roll a very soft ball of paperclay between your palms. Push into it with a thumb or forefinger to open it up.

Pinching seems simple but there are nuances to get the walls to be even that take a little practice.

Pinch the sides of the hole evenly until the walls of the little bowl gradually thin out as seen to right. Try to keep the walls even pinching in a consistent rhythm. And control the pinch so you don't pinch too much, too little, or too close, or too far etc. So make sets as much as possible for practice will really pay off.

Another help is to rotate the little bowl around after each pinch. Keep the hand above and the palm steady. I don't pinch the top lip of the pot so much. I let the lip stay little thicker until the final touches. Also, for a shine after it dries, burnish or rub the hardened outside surface with the back of a spoon, shell, or river rock.

The burnish feature is the same as traditional clay except paperclay holds up better when it is bone dry. Also, a chance to alter, assemble, or repair by wet on dried states is open to you.

Press with a Steady Rhythm: *To gradually thin the soft walls evenly, rotate the pot a little between pinches. Aim to press consistently the same each time.*

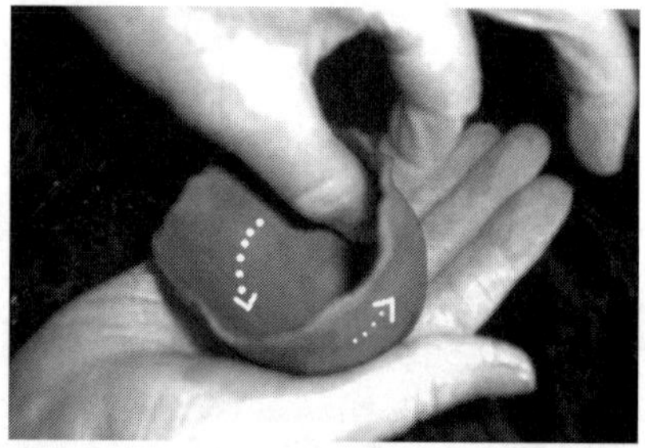

Figure Studies

Try thumbnail sketch studies with paperclay for a warm up. Start with as soft ball of P'Clay and fast pinch what will start off looking like a heavy "5 point star" but keep going. Pinch one point of the star for a head, and make the arms and legs out of the rest. Crimp the ends for feet and hands. Though the result or "study" is still lumpy looking, the sense of a figure in a mime of a "Clay Clown" is starting to be visible. Repeat until you have multiple figures. Note how each fresh one is faster and easier than the one before. Allow a minute or two each and the clay never has any time to stiffen too much. Put the figures in a little groups suggesting activity such as a dance, a marching group, musicians, a classroom, a dinner table, a sport team huddle, gymnasts, circus, ballet, etc. Rest floppy figures to stiffen dry on a side. Use a bit of scrap to temporarily prop wild arms, or legs. At bone dry, for practice with joins, try gluing some together in circles, or acrobat towers like in a circus with P'Slip. Or detail some mini-masks to add over the faces, or props, hats etc., or take off, at the bone dried state. The variations are endless. Dress them with unknown glaze for test fires. If you planned the test glaze to be a "clown" suit from the beginning, even the ugliest surprise glaze could pass for OK.

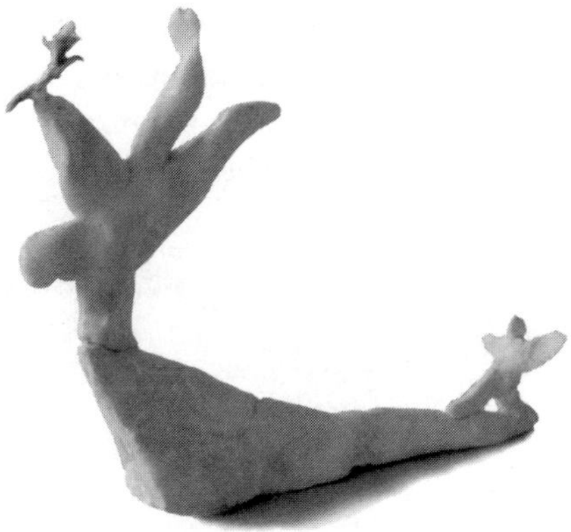

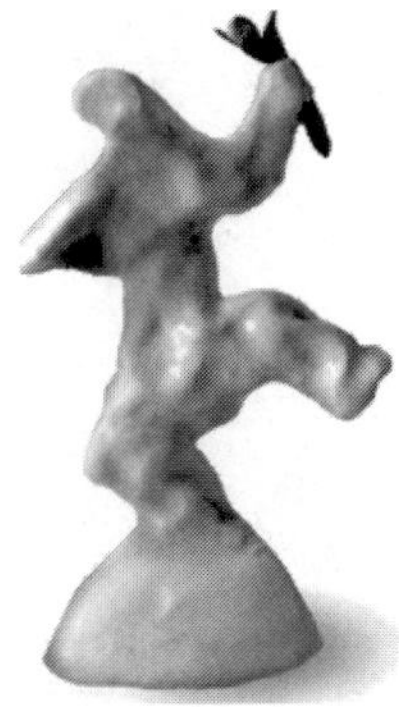

***"Clay Clown Figures"** by author. On the right, look for the "upside down bowl" and the abstract "5 end points of the star" mentioned in the text above. Balance the bone dried "easy to handle" figure upright on top the bone dry "pedestal" with generous dabs of P'Slip as adhesive.*

Medallion or Hand Tile

Flatten a soft clay ball into a small hamburger patty or shape. Use the table top to help if you don't have a rolling pin. Just flip the patty over and over several time. To keep clay from sticking to the table, try moving to a to a new dry area on the table. Use sharp pencils as scribes. Make scribble marks and carve lines, dots, zig-zags, and so forth. For instant texture: press in tree leaves, woven lace, fabric, or even paper doilies. To poke a perfect hole for hanging later, try the end of larger plastic drinking straw. At bone dry, wipe clear any stray 'nips' with a moist sponge. For a quick good looking finish either at bone dried or at fired, stain the surface with the edge of a wet sponge full of a dark colored clay slip, glaze, water or acrylic color. Then, rub or clean wipe some of the color off the top with a fresh damp sponge. The dark stain will have seeped down in the pre-scribed lines or the textures. Instantly, turn all scratch marks and even scribbles and textures into clean borderlines this way. Shoe polish can work, but it stains hands. Next, Its easy and neat looking to color between the "lines" with water or acrylic like a coloring book. For a non-fire finish, brush a seal coat of white glue thinned 50/50 with water.

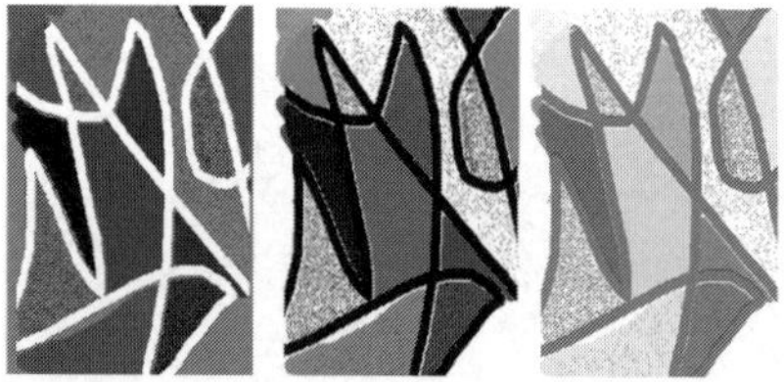

Fig. 14: ***Like a Coloring Book:*** *Scribe a doodle with a toothpick in the soft P'Clay surface of a flat hand patty, rolled tile, pinch pot, or etc. Leave the rough scratch to harden overnight. Next work session, P'Clay is dry. It's far easier to wipe off the dry debris leftover from the doodle, and the lines to color in stay neat and crisp. Three different variations for "coloring" in the same doodle are shown on the left.*

Learning Curve

Clay goes through changes over time. It is half solid and half fluid. It is not what it first appears to be. Like all ceramic make friends with it gradually over time Follow the new piece of paperclay back and forth between wet and dry states and through fire. Get to know what you can do best with it at each state.

When traditional clay is introduced, weeks, months, or years later, the prior experience with P'Clay has set the stage for more success in traditional discipline. The ability to secure joins and handle parts will be a habit to carry over easily by then.

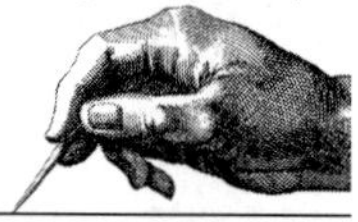

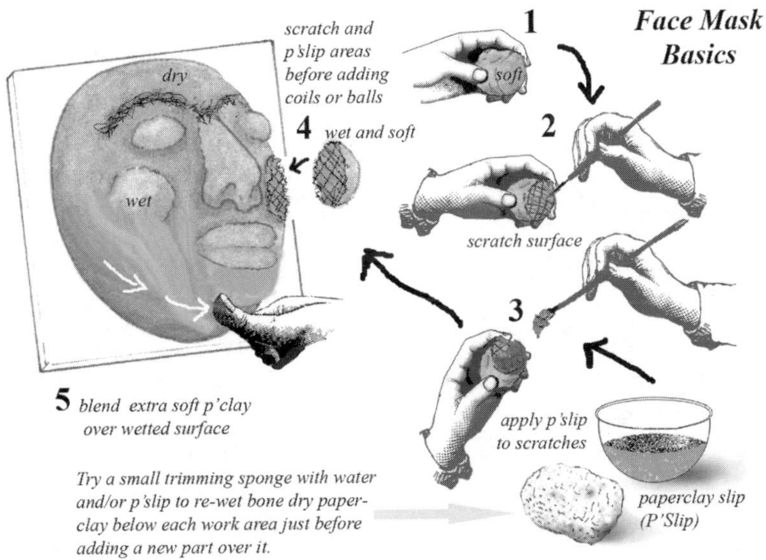

Faces and Masks

Blend soft wads into the mask surface the same way you might in traditional clay. The big difference is the mask surface you work over can be totally hard and bone dried. One can re-wet the bone dried with a damp sponge multiple times. In fact many find that a totally dried shell works far better to start with than a leather hard one.

Many like that the paperclay dries hard enough for working it in a comfortable angle on a lap or table and then attaching the detailed parts after. Paperclay does not need babying or slow drying the way traditional clays usually do. Figure 15 on the left can give you some idea of where to start practicing faces with it.

Fig. 15: ***Contour Modeling:*** *A hard and totally dry paperclay mask or shell won't break or deform easily as you work over it. Re-wet spot work areas with a sponge just before joining or merging fresh new soft P'Clay over. Scratch surfaces to be joined with needle tool or fork or sharp pencil, dab a bit of water or P'Slip, press together, and then, blend contours in with fingers or tools. To trim the finish at bone dry, maybe carve some highlight definition to contour of lips, eyes, nose, ears, with a fettle knife or needle.*

Classroom Tips

A typical bag of 25 lbs. of soft P'Clay ceramic paperclay will serve a class of thirty with extra to spare. Light color clays are better. Dark clays tend to stain hands and/or clothing. Close the remainder clay in the bag with a tablespoon of water. Soft P'Clay exposed to dry air stiffens too hard to model with. P'Slip is a water slurry of P'Clay mashed with fork or fingers in a cup. It is most often used as a glue and seal for dried parts. Discourage mushing leftover or overworked P'Clay back into hard balls that resist slaking down or recycling. P'Clays should be used fresh. Refuse to fire student works until they pass muster. Handles should be well-attached, the work wiped clean when its dry with a little damp sponge, and signed with initials, mark, date, year etc.

Whether to Fire

All properly balanced mix of ceramic paperclay or P'Clay can survive kiln fire. If time to fire "disappears," or if a kiln is not available, then finish with out one as follows. Give the works a quick coat of seal (such as white glue and water mixed 50/50) to set the surface. The works can be stained and sponged to show off textures in a jiffy. Acrylic paint, nail polish, or even, buffed up car wax, might suit. Send non-fired projects home to hang on the wall, or sit on a bookshelf. as memento. Air dry work may be super simple one color, or be dotted, striped and etc. If no kiln is involved, may be incorporate items like sequins, feathers, paperclips, rubber bands, toothpicks, string and beads.

For watertight dish-safe paperclay ware then a glaze fire in kilns is required.

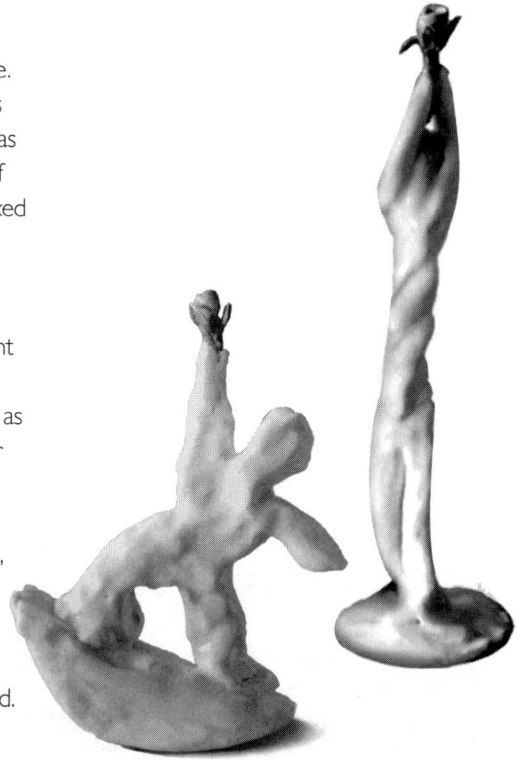

Rosette Gault

Chapter two

Studio Basics

2

Wedging and Preparation

> **Clay "Words" New to You?**
>
> Traditional modeling clay is a half solid-half fluid mix of clay (microscopic flat mineral chips pictured on page 81) and water. If clay is watered down into a slurry, it is called **slip**. (For shorthand, I added a prefix of "P" to the original words to quickly refer to paper clay versions) As water evaporates, soft clay turns **leatherhard,** and ultimately turns solid at **bone dry**, or **greenware state,** before fire. The oven for clay ware is a **kiln.** Water seeps through the shape of unglazed semi-fired **Bisque or Biscuit** ware. More terms clay workers use are in the glossary is on page 131.

Is it necessary to wedge before use?

If you have a bag of pugged P'Clay®, skip the wedging steps described in the next question. You paid for the convenience of a ready soft and homogenous chunk to start work with.

Kneading, or "wedging," air pockets out of studio made paper clay is a matter of personal "preference" not a technical need. A paper clay is much more "open" compared to traditional clay. If you are a beginner, or intermediate, learning the wheel, the feel of an air bubble in the wall of the pot might put you, or your pot, off center.

Paper clays are ***far*** less likely to blow apart in the first fire than a traditional ware. Explosions of paper clay in the kiln could happen if one first turns on the heat in a cold kiln, and then, neglects to give any trapped residues of interior water vapor steam ***enough TIME to escape via the network of cellulose fiber paths*** (i.e. between 150 to 212F). Leatherhard ***low*** pulp, or very thick paper clay pieces are the most vulnerable. Steam also forms inside traditional clays at the "first" heating of the form as the temperature rises through the boiling point of water (about 212F).

What is an easy way to prepare or wedge the clay if I want to?

If I have a bucket of P'Slip on hand, I sponge out any excess water from the top of the mix, and then spread the mud-like paper clay over plaster slabs, drying tubs, or bats. Let the puddle dry to desired soft consistency. Find a a picture of the "puddle" on page 27. Scrape up the soft set paperclay with a rubber rib as soon as its ready. If the paper clay is too dry, wedging will be difficult. High pulp clay dries a little quicker, and can feel a little like putty to wedge.

Can I cut wedged paper clay easily with a wire or a needle?

Yes, a wedged paper clay body, with a short fiber cellulose pulp explained in Chapter 5, can be sliced clean apart with a wire, or needle, provided it is not too dried and stiff.

Can I coil with paper clay?

Whether by means of a "rock and roll" rhythm on a table, or by hand squeezing, make soft P'Clay into "ropes" of any diameter or length. Assemble and coil these 'end-to-end' to build up vessel or sculptural forms. Spiral and corkscrew based structures are most common. There is no need to mush, or score, the paper clay "coils" together as would be required with a traditional clay. Should you take advantage of the freedom of "wet on dry," coil on and on "without a care" as detailed in the last chapter.

After the form dries and hardens completely, a "seal in the gaps" step makes more sense. Brush or putty in P'Slip between the coil lines, as much, or as little, as you want. Dip an entire bone dry coil pot in the bucket of P'Slip to get an instant seal coat in every corner all at once. Smooth, or wipe off the excess with a damp sponge. The seal chore is completed and you could be done. But for many of use this just leads to an optional added chance to improvise with new coils building on up over the dried ones from there. Find more variations as you read on.

P'Slip for Touch Ups and PATCH

Stir and mash soft P'Clay® in a cup with water until lumps are gone and voila! A simple P'Slip is ready. Simple P'Slip is adhesive enough without need of any extras like vinegar, or etc.

Can I make pinch pots with paper clay?

Yes, but start off with soft clay. Let the clay "air stiffen" as you go along, and there is no limit. The previous chapter shows some pictures of pinch figures, but there are many variations.

Can I get smooth surfaces, even burnished surfaces?

Yes, tiny paper fibers at the surface, barely visible to the naked eye, may be burnished smooth with a finger, rib tool, or stone. I use a soft rubber rib to smooth any canvas or table textures off the top of my fresh made slabs.

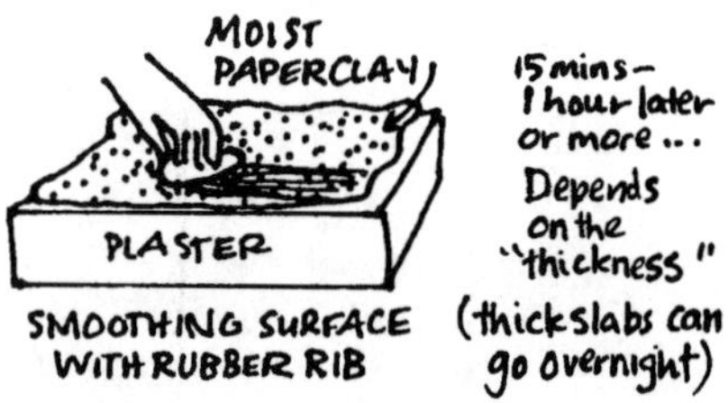

The more I burnish or rub a paper clay, the more I compress the fibers on the surface similar to the fibers shown on page 79. As the clay stiffens up, a patina shine will form. To join over burnished areas, scratch or scrape off the burnish for a good adhesion.

Don't the fibers show?

No, if by chance I notice a clump of unsaturated fiber on the surface, it's easy to pick it out and smooth the pock over before firing. If I notice too many clumps of unsaturated paper fibers in your paper clay, in the next batch, use hotter water and/or strain or screen your pulp several times before adding it to the clay. Fibers in pulp should be so well dispersed in the liquid clay slip that they are not obvious.

Tile and Slab Construction

Can I roll the P'Clay flat out like pie or cookie dough for a tile or slab?

Absolutely, and cut tile to any shape after that, as per photos on pages 29 and 30. More on giant size special purpose slabs will be explained in the next chapter on life scale projects.

A beginner intermediate could practice as follows: First, flatten the paper clay ball between the palms into a large flat patty. Use a kitchen style rolling pin over top the thick pancake shape. Roll over this several times with a consistent and gentle to medium pressure. Flip the patty over to a dry spot on the table every few rollovers so it thins more, but doesn't stick. In this way, the new slab will form more evenly as the table surface, and periodic turnovers help keep lumps at a minimum. Place two equal sized flat sticks vertically at the sides of clay. Rollover them at the same time. This limits the thinness of the slab to the limit of the stick size.

Can I use paper clay in a slab roller or extruder?

Yes, but it's easier if the slab is close to the flatness you want first. Softer paper clay is needed to extrude, too. Paper clay seems to stiffen up at a variable rate with these big tools.
I rarely use a slab roller because a plaster drying slab gives me a uniform depth, no disturbance of clay particle alignment, and thus, exact control over finish results. The next chapter details more on this.

Can I bend and alter paper clay slabs?

Yes, be sure the slab is quite moist when you do this. Five minutes can make a difference with tight angled graceful curves and rolls. Depending on how much pulp and moisture you have, the slab will seem less stretchy than the parent clay would. Nonetheless, if you bend too far, and crack the slab surface by accident, it's easy enough to repair and fill in later. Also, dip, or soak, bone dry slabs in water to soften them again. These will curve "some" without a crack, but they can not bend the same as they could when freshly formed. Refer to pages 47-49 for more about this. Practice and you will succeed in slab skill.

Can I throw with paper clay on the wheel?

Potter's Blend P'Clays® are now available pugged in bags for beginners, intermediates, and up. Chapter 4 Conventional clays work best on the wheel for bowls and simple forms.
It will not be easy to make a good throwing body using the directions in this book. Nevertheless, Sculptor's P'Clay® is good on a wheel. For large or complex wheel forms, it might serve you right. Instantly, studio batch generates copious amounts of slurry. Trimming will dull your tools in a hurry. See Chapter 4 for details..

Can I use paper clay "slip" to join parts together?
Yes, it makes a stronger joint than regular slip. Reserve some of the mud from the mixing barrel in Chapter 6 for later use as an adhesive. I call this material P'Slip, as explained earlier.

What's the best way to join two larger dry parts together?
Wet the dry areas with generous amounts of P'Slip and putty each end with some plastic paper clay. Smooth out, score, and join the softer wet ends together with more P'Slip per below. See more about join reinforcement later in this chapter.

Do the parts have to be of equal thickness?
No, thick (2" or so) is fine next to thin (1/4" or so) in most cases. The more pulp in your recipe the more grace you have.

What is the dry strip method?
Make a set of concentric circles with coils or strips that can be stacked on top of each other "dry," and then sealed together with wet P'Slip or soft P'Clay. Smear P'Slip liberally to the surfaces for textural effect as Ann Sanders in her "Drum" on page 129.

How might I build a freestanding structure such as a torso?
Make up some rolls, hollow tubes, or coils, of paper clay in different sizes. The hollow rolls are strongest.

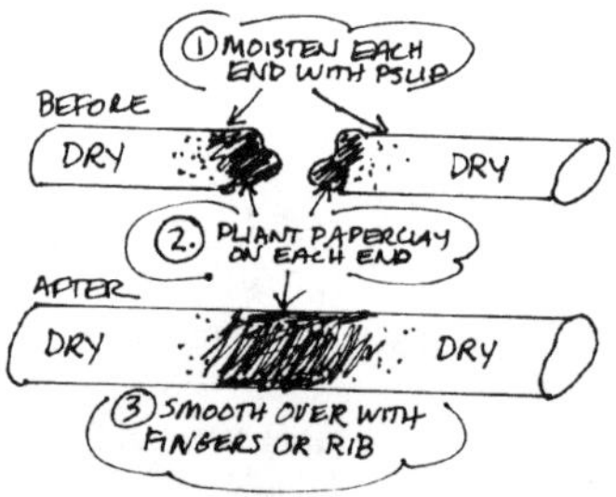

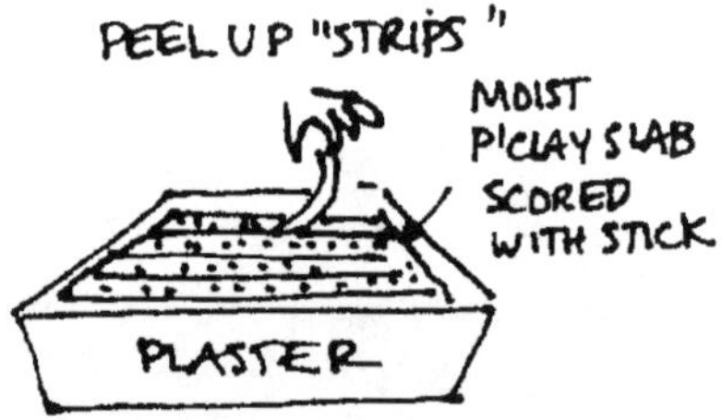

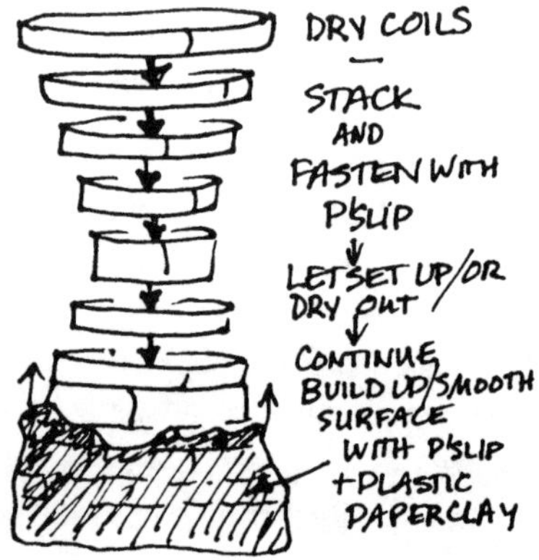

Bend them as you like to form the gestures of the body. Let these dry out overnight. Next day, assemble a basic armature out of these tubes using wet and plastic paper clay to join the ends together smoothly. If that does not look right, break off an arm deliberately, and reattach it in a new position with more paper clay. Maybe drape some thin slabs, wet, dry, or damp, over the top. Later, after the form has dried out, add more thicknesses of wet or plastic paper clay to build up muscles, or to round, and smooth out the surfaces.

How might I model a face or figure? For the head, improvise a paper clay a globe structure out of dried curved paper clay strips. I also can coil build or cast two oval bowls and let them dry. I would assemble them rim to rim; putty in gaps with wet over dry; and then, fill in where the muscles and tissue should be. Suppose I want to change the features on a dry face I modeled yesterday. I add a fresh layer of wet and/or plastic paper clay over top, and continue where I left off. If I change my mind *again* tomorrow, that's OK, too. I add as many layers as I require. The combined depth could probably be as much about

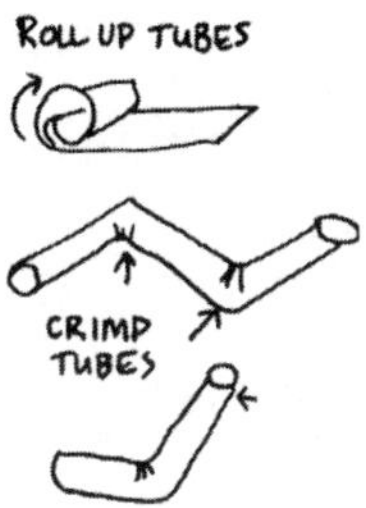

Armature Parts: *Roll-up quick rough un-trimmed "tubes" and let harden all the way dry. Armature supports built with these will be strong, hollow for flexion in drying and firing.*

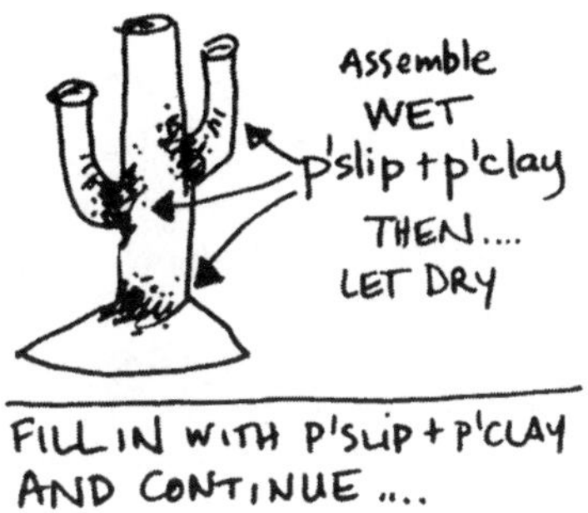

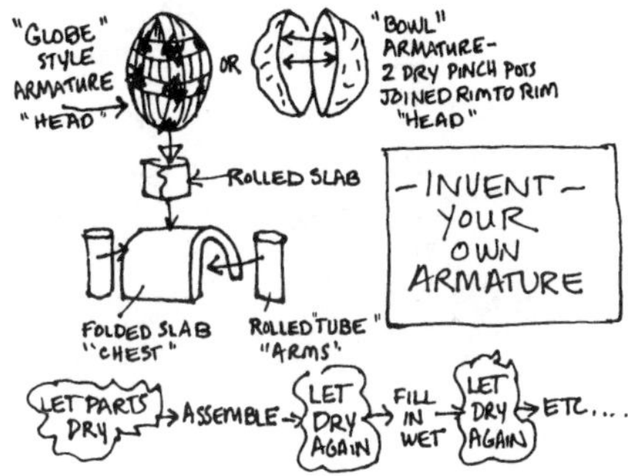

3," or so, and the layers do not have to be even. To model and build up detail refer to the illustration on page 23. For a shortcut, see the photos on page 68. I like the opportunity to model or carve details over bone dry segments **in my lap.** I position the face, head, hand, or other part, at an angle which is most comfortable for me. I periodically return the part to it's intended place upon the figure whenever I want to see how the intended assembly looks from a distance.

Can I insert small sculptural fragments of already fired bisqued or glazed ceramic into the wet paper clay, and then fire them intact?
I do this when it would be right for the sculpture. "Insertions" may, or may not, be made of paper clay. Small items of greenware could also be used. I inserted miniature thrown glazed pots and small sculptures made of conventional clay directly into the wet. I fired all of this assembled with success.

To make a paste of P'Slip, think ahead when mixing pulp with clay slip so you add enough, but not too much, water to either the pulp or the slip from the start, as Chapter 6 explains in detail. Or just wait. In time, a runny P'Slip naturally turns into paste in the bucket, if left uncovered and stirred every now and then. On plaster, in certain weather, watch it more closely. Again, timing of this is key.

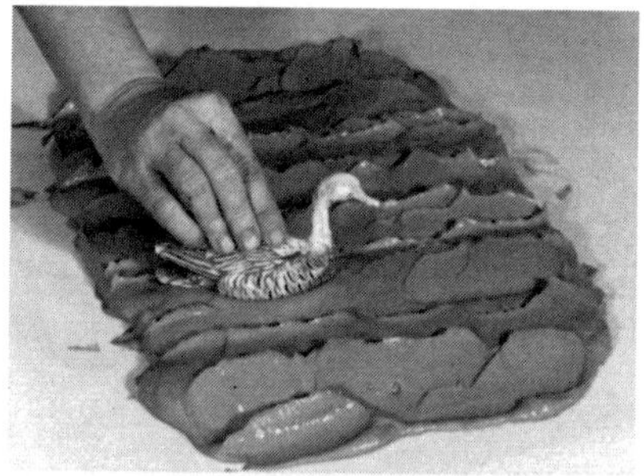

Fig. 24: ***Insertion of Bone Dried or Fired Ceramic****: When P'Slip thickens to a paste, like "icing," waves are easy to make. Ease wave up with a rib or spatula. On the surface of a bone dried cast duck, it was easy to scratch needle fine "feather texture" and under-cut new definition and detail. After bisque fire of the duck, to highlight the texture, I sponge-rubbed the body with a watered down dark stain that seeped in my cut and trim lines. All glaze coats were pre-applied to the duck before the insertion. The wet clay waves dried up around the duck with no crack, and both fired together intact.*

Carving

Can I carve on paper clay?

Yes, carve paper clay quite easily when soft, or before it is leather hard. Carvers who are used to traditional clay may not like how stiff, short, and hard to cut through leatherhard state paper clay is. Since leatherhard state clay has not finished shrinking its not the ideal stage to work on or carve. Bone dried may be better for some forms. To remedy stiffness, re-wet the work area with a sponge and wait several minutes for the surface to soften. Most times, the entire dry form can be dipped in water to soften it for more carving.

To get "super crisp" detail, try sintering or pre-firing the form to 1000 F, which is just enough heat to destroy the cellulose fibers within. A sintered clay, especially if it is porcelain, or a fine grained 'ball and talc' body, carves off as a powder. Most sintered forms can still take additional layers of fresh P'Clay as well. Experiment. Be aware that as the paper fibers are burned away, the classic rules of clay may apply again. Forms that have been sintered can then be fired to normal higher temperatures afterward.

*Fig. 25: **Crisp, Clean, Smooth, Trim Carving:** Remember the porcelain crisp carving surface that has no fiber or grit at all? Get it. Burn paper fibers out of the paperclay in an ultra low temperature "sinter" fire, then carve. Sintered porcelain can be less fragile to carve on. The finish result compares to a plaster master. Clean machine trims of sintered paperclay are also possible by lathe, Dremel detail tool, blade or the like.*

How easy is it to model detail?

Provided paper clay is not too dry, you can achieve fine detail as you would with the traditional clay it was based on. Re-soften bone dried details with a damp sponge if you want or need to..

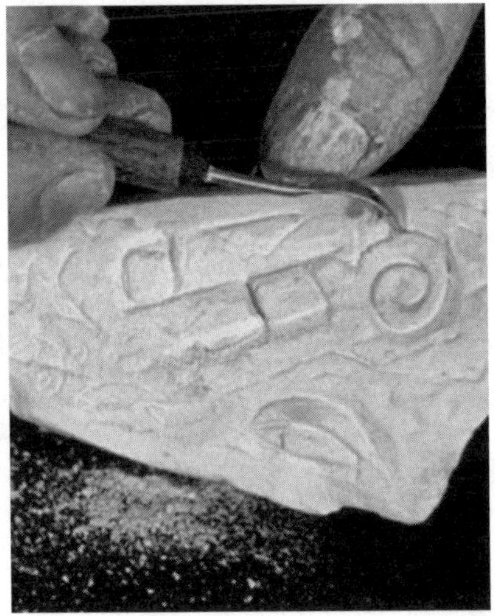

Cutting

Can I cut 'cookie cutter' shapes?
Yes, leathersoft moist slabs are easiest to cut by pointed stick, or needle, as seen in the photos on pages 29 and 30. For bone dry cuts, consider a jigsaw, or even a power tool.

How do I cut paper clay when it has dried out?
One method is to score a line with a needle tool where you want the break to be, and gently and slowly apply pressure until the dry paper clay breaks apart. Most of the time, the break will be along the line you made. Smooth the edge with a wet sponge. If cutting a large slab, it is much like cutting glass: score and snap apart. Hand or power tools may also be used.

Pre-score intended cutlines lines in the soft slab with a needle. I do not pierce all the way through. Snapping off the excess can be easier at bone dry, particularly with flat tile. There is less drag on the saw blade if less paperclay to cut through.

Plan for the same two "shrinkage episodes" in paper clay as in traditional clay. In very "tight" installs of tile, for example, cutting to measure after "phase one" shrinkage has finished (bone dry) reduces the chance of calculation errors if measuring at wet or leather hard. Learn why shrinkage is a valuable asset for building with paper clay in Chapter 3.

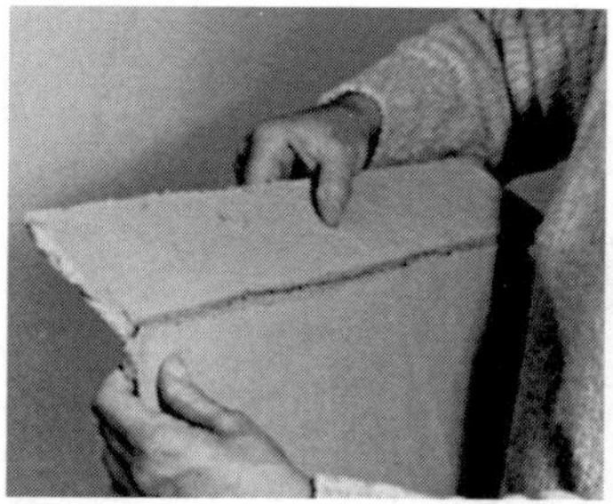

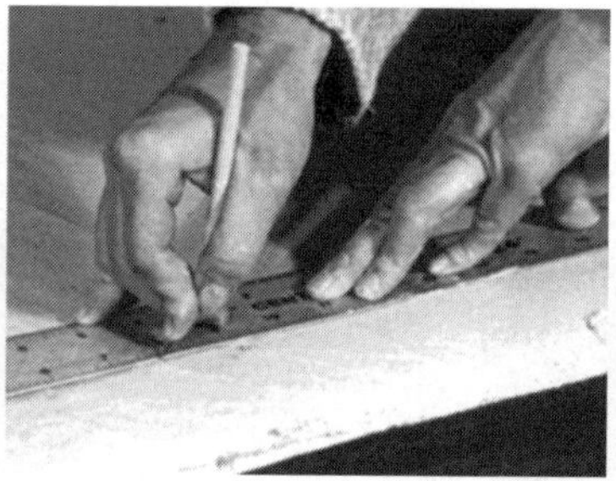

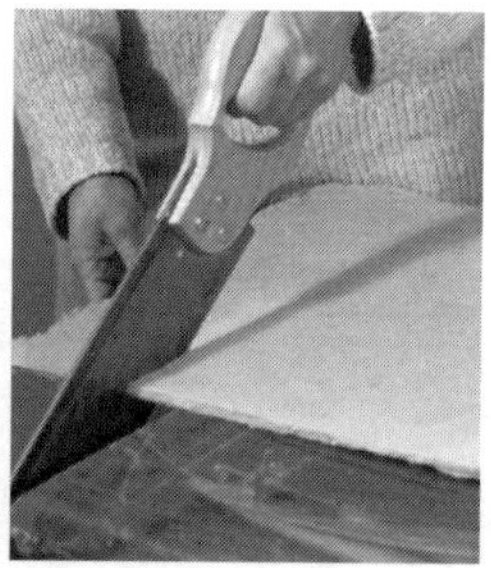

Score and Cut Greenware: *Score a cut line with a needle. Snap apart like glass. Maybe use power jig or handsaw for box parts, etc. This board of flat paperclay dried totally over plaster uncovered. See page 47 for detail on preparation.*

Slabs

Is it possible to make a very large flat slab that does not warp?

Large slabs of wet paper clay, made from P'Slip poured over a well made absorbent plaster surface, do not warp, if handled properly. After a few hours, or the next day, gently lift the super soft slab up "once." See the photo below. When you put the slab back down, a microscopic layer of air reduces friction from underneath as it dried. This is explained in further detail on pages 47-49. Study the slab chart on page 47, too. If this is done, most slabs, no matter how thin, will not stick to the plaster, or warp. Slabs normally dry out evenly in contact with a "properly made" plaster. If you think your bone dry flat slab is too thin, and, it still rests on a plaster surface, simply spread out a fresh layer of wet P'Slip directly over top the dry as thick as you want Multiple layerings are good, in general. The first time I made figure sized slabs (5 ft. x 2 ft. about 80 cm x 120 cm). I set them up on a linoleum floor of the studio over newspaper because there was no plaster surface to use. Ten days of drying and frequent turnovers were required. If the weather had been humid, drying could have been taken a month! During the process, the paper clay was getting drier and less plastic. I bent a slab too far, and started a crack. Not to worry. The dry crack was completely healed with P'Slip and moist paper clay at the bone dry stage. Most repairs before bone dry are

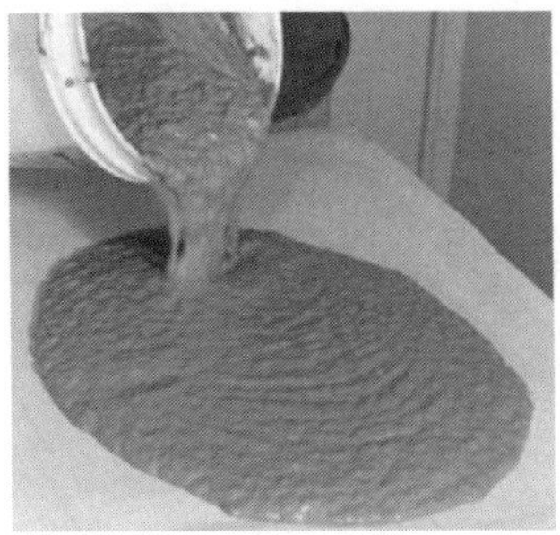

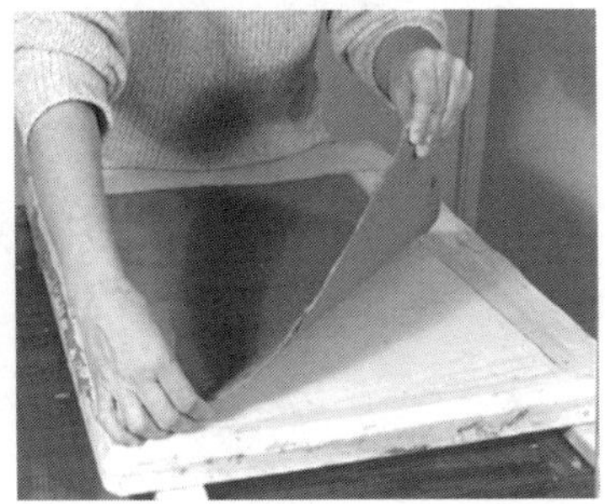

Fig. 27A left side: ***Pour P'Slip over Plaster****. Just as the surface stops "shining" either: a. scrape it up to keep as soft P'Clay, or: b. wait, then to release peel off a uniform leather soft thick "page" as in Fig. 27B to right. If I lift too soon, the slab will stick to the plaster in places and tear. After the release, set the leathersoft flat on plaster to dry completely flat. Or, to bend or roll a tube without surface cracking, roll up when leathersoft. Wipe very dry plaster down with a damp sponge before starting a pour.*

Template for Flat Shapes to Fold Up into Armature Parts

1. From a paperclay sheet, cut-out a big flat cookie like shape. Run thumb along periphery of your cutout to bevel a smooth clean edge.

2. If floppy or limp, let slab set up a bit in open air until it just stiffens enough to fold it without cracking its surface. If you wait too long it will get too stiff to fold and stand up easily.

3. Fold cutout shapes up in "tent" forms as suggested below.

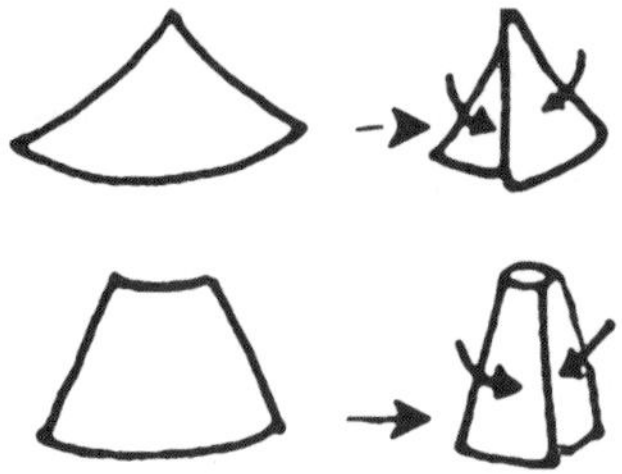

Hollow "cone" designs for armature parts with pointed or tapered ends. Possible starts for arms, legs, trees, sticks, branches, etc.

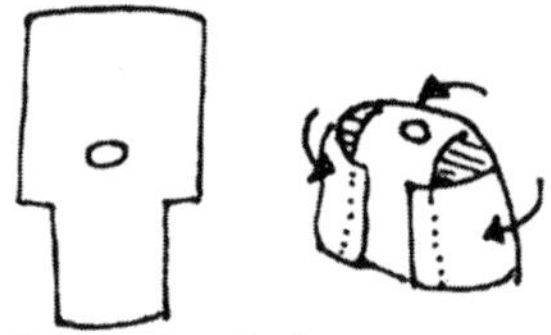

Pattern for a hollow armature.

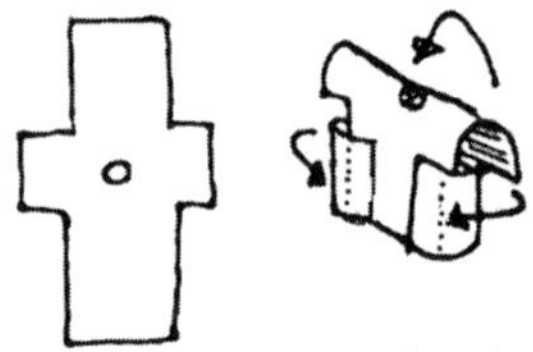

Pattern for an "upper torso" armature.

*Assemble or build over these **when totally dry** at the maximum possible stability, durability, and hardness. These "instant" armatures are inspired by origami, or fabric patterns.*

Avoid carving out the insides of leatherhard paperclay.

Hollow structures dry more quickly, survive temperature change better and weigh less.

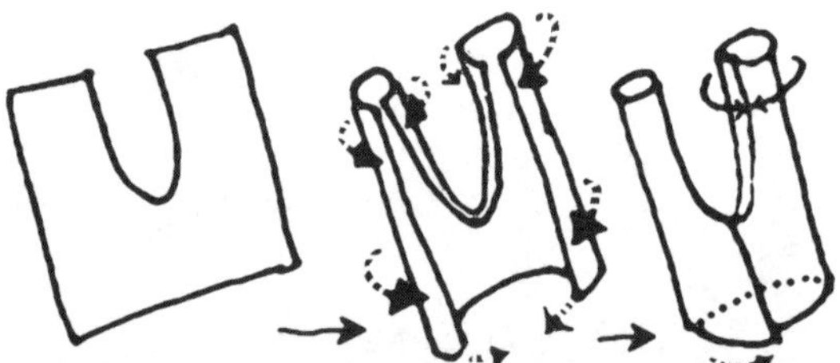

"Legs to Stand On" Pattern.

Bend "pant leg" edges up and in for a quick lower torso armature

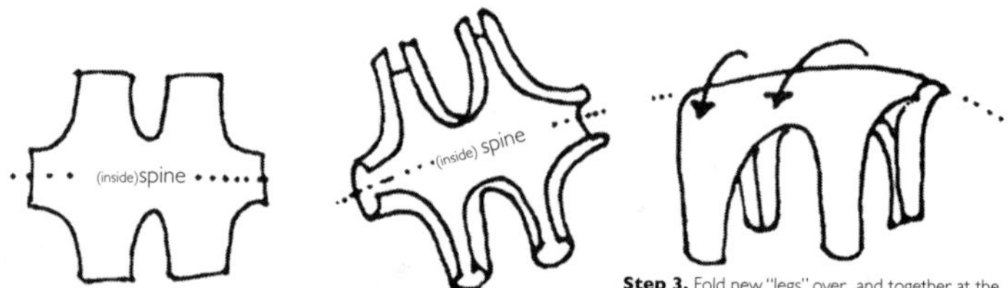

Step 1: Cut pattern in soft clay sheet.

Step 2: Prepare the inside legs before standing body up, first, fold each leg into a curl as shown

Step 3. Fold new "legs" over and together at the spine line. Stand the structure upright. Adapt and crimp legs to gesture before hardening. Fill in open gaps at bone dry. Then, attach some new parts: head, feet, tail, ears and etc.

Pattern to Start a "Four Legged Animal."

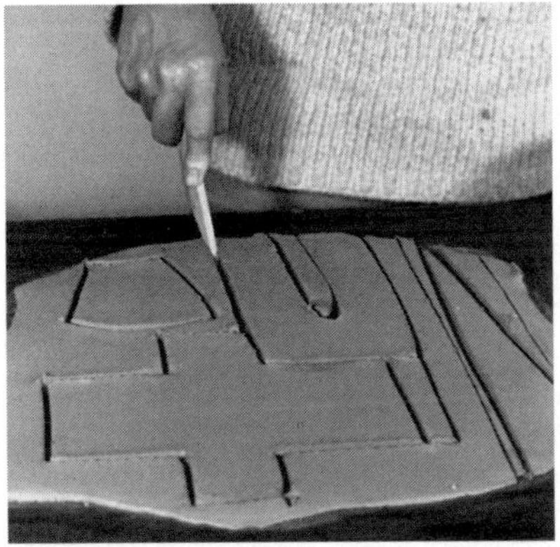

Fig. 29A: ***Armature Cut-outs:***
Drag a sharp stick across the soft surface of leathersoft paperclay to make outlines of simple (or complex) template shapes. As the moist clay stiffens up in the air a bit, fold these into freestanding hollow curves. Diagrams to left, page 28, show my designs for simple armature shapes to try out. At bone dry, the sturdy result can either be built over, or finished and trimmed as is.

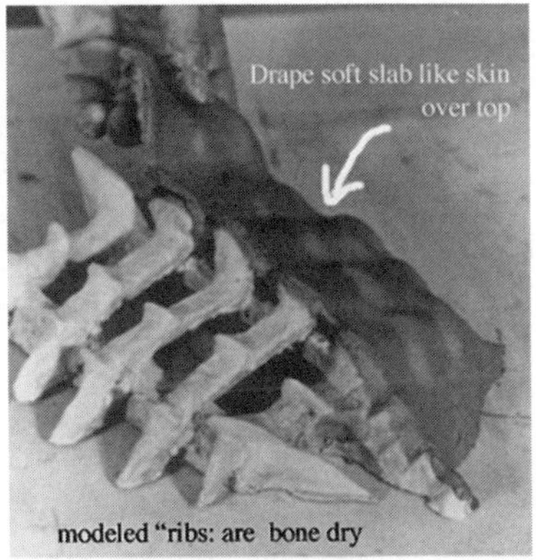

Fig. 29B: ***Skin Fits over Bones:***
Drape leather soft slabs, as if a fabric, over a bone dry form to take a 3D "print" of the contour. After the slab hardens, lift the new shape off. If you are working large scale and want to attach the skin to the bone. Wait and let the skin dry completely first. It will shrink without resistance. Then with wet on dry, fit the dried hard skin to the dried bones. Skeleton by author.

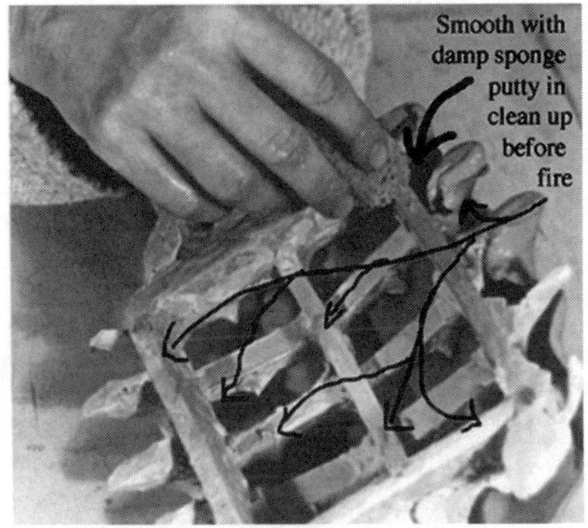

Fig. 29C: ***Trim and Reinforce Underneath:***
Give the "undersides" of your sculptures attention before the first fire. Clean up, putty, sponge down, and trim to perfection everywhere. The complex edges in the support structure is easily covered over too. When done, the underneath will look and feel as finished as the top.

not worth the trouble. Thick areas next to thin areas also survived my repeated tests without cracks.

Wall mural tiles have been made en masse by pouring P'Slip out over doubled sheets of plaster drywall. See tiles on pages 129-130. Cut or scribe some crisp edge guidelines while tiles are still soft with a needle and ruler. Check the air drafts in the space and turn the tiles until dry. Plasterboard or drywall is not quite as effective as plaster for flat drying, but it's better compared to the surface of a floor.

Flat slabs can even be fired with success when bridged across kiln shelves. Size of the kiln, not the kiln shelf, is the ultimate limit for works constructed in paper clay and fired intact. Sprinkle some sand on the kiln shelves underneath larger slabs or sculptures to reduce chance of cracks during the firing due to excess friction as the works can expand and contract in the fire. This matter will be explained further in the next chapter.

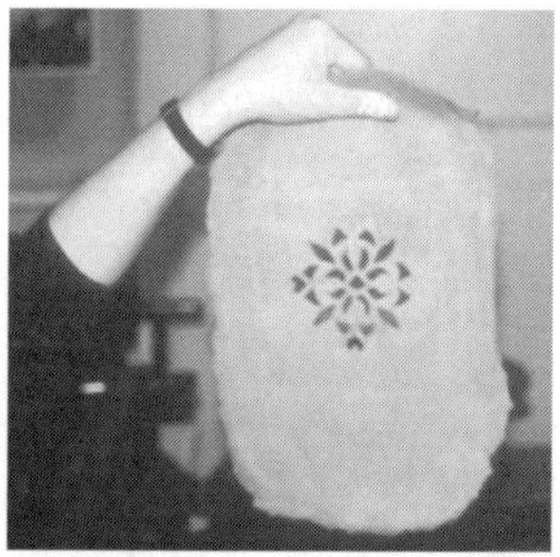

Fig. 30: ***Leathersoft Resembles Fabric:*** *Dangle (gently!) a thin "leathersoft" paper clay slab in mid-air and it remains intact. Cutout detail of see-through holes is in progress. Trim with damp sponge when dry.*

Mending

What about repairs and cracks?

When accidents or cracks happen, repairs to paper clay are simple. Fill in and putty around the crack, or weak area, with both wet and plastic paper clay right over top of the dry. Students report repairs of cracked bisque mended and fired again with P'Slip!

I repaired a miniature broken finger atop a bisqued "hand" made of terra cotta P'Clay. The new finger attached

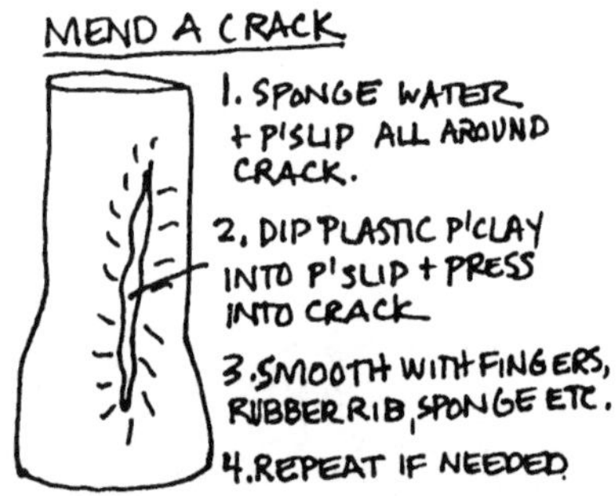

to the bisque ware stump, and it survived fire with out cracks! ***If you have already lost a piece, then what else can you lose by trying a repair?*** Again, knowledge of your base clay is essential. Success is far more likely if you wet the bisque with water first, then apply a coat of thinned P'Slip, and then model with soft P'Clay on top of that. Chapter 5 has more "success keys." Re- bisque the joins that dried well to check them, before high fire.

Why is it that mending with paper clay tends not to crack?

As a crack starts in the clay, cellulose fibers absorb and interrupt the path. Also, the curly-q roots of fiber resist being pulled out of their tracks. This will explained more on pages 85-89.

Can I use different batches of paper clay together?

Yes, if the maturing temperatures of each paper clay are "similar," bonds will hold up through a firing.

Are there good ways to repair broken "legs" or "arms"?

"Legs" usually support the entire weight of the sculpture, not just before the firing, but long after, the paper fibers are gone. The strongest possible repairs are recommended to reinforce such structures. The better strategy is to sculpt increased surface area on both sides of the break, let

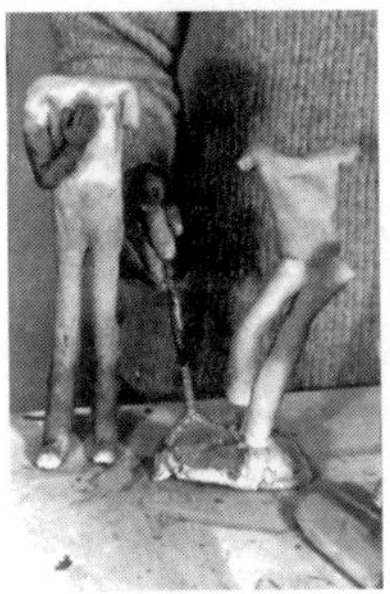

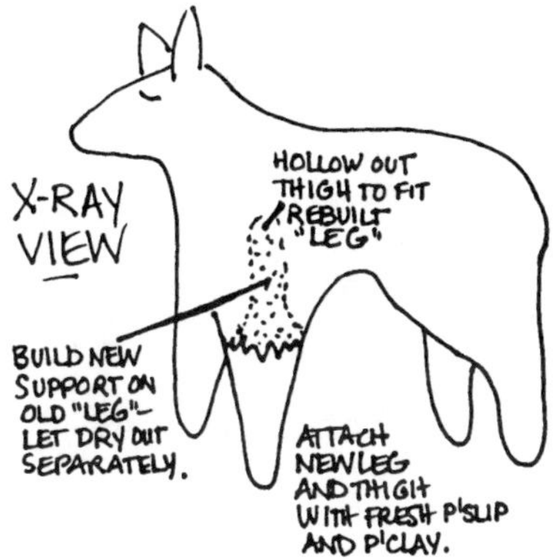

Fig. 31 A and B: ***Plan to Reinforce Weight Bearing Joins:*** *Dark areas in photo are wet, light areas are dried. Use a fan brush to generously apply P'Slip to the bone dry part before modeling P'Clay on top or in between. Multiple drying intervals help. Legs and feet must support the weight of figure above them through the fire. For example, "reinforce" weight bearing joins in the "legs" more attentively than others. Internal pins of dried paperclay can sometimes serve as hidden stabilizers.*

both sides dry out before re-wetting and joining again, as shown in the dog illustration on the previous page.

Step One: on the shorter piece: sculpt an appendage off the stump, and, on the larger side: drill or hollow out a receptacle to fit. Step Two: assemble the dried out parts using P'Slip and P'Clay as usual for joining wet on dry parts.

What if I want extra reinforcement on a joint or vulnerable part of my form?

Use several layers of P'Slip, applied in opposite directions, over top of the leather hard or dry part. This has the effect of interweaving and braiding layers of fibers over of each other like a custom fitting fabric over curves in your paper clay armature. Imagine a custom fit "fluid plywood laminate."

Can I use paper clay strips for patch bandages?

Dip-coat strips or cutouts of any size, texture, or shape, of fresh leather condition P'Clay in a bucket of P'Slip. Then, apply them as "patches," or bandages, inside, or outside, your form as an alternative to coils or direct application of P'Slip. If the form is bone dry, and has been moistened slightly with a sponge a few moments beforehand, most patches stick right away.

Can I control the "grain" or direction of the fiber in my paper clay form?

Wet fibers in the slurry can, more or less, be lined up in a consistent direction with your fingers, serrated rib, or a comb. Control the deposit of fibers by attention to factors such as: a.) the number, alignment, and shape of the 'teeth' in the comb used, and b.) the base clay and pulp recipe chosen.

What if I want to increase the fired strength of a high loft paper clay?

Use layers of different concentrations (of pulp) paper clay, one over top the other. Vary the composition and melting points of various blends of P'Slip. To lower the maturing point of the P'Slip, and make it even more "glue-like" in the kiln fire, add a small bit of extra "glaze." Or, for an opposite stabilizing effect, add a bit more alumina, ball clay, or china clay instead. Armatures with higher melting points could be built beneath a thin walled high flux porcelain to lend further support from within. These could be certain to stand the heat, for example. Use casting slip for the base clay, and get closer alignment and density of clay particles if your project calls for this level of precision.

Also, try Daniel Rhode's system of dipping fiberglass cloth in paper clay slip, and making an additional internal layer of fiberglass, that will fuse to the clay if the firing reaches a high enough temperature. It is possible to apply the dipped fiberglass cloth strips wet over dry paper clay, provided the area below is re-moistened with a damp sponge first. Simple bandages of P'Clay may meet your need without the extra trouble of fiberglass. Read more about use of fluff fiberglass or spun alumina fiber dispersed in porcelain P'Slip in some recent journal articles listed on page 120.

Alignment of Cellulose Fibers in Slurry

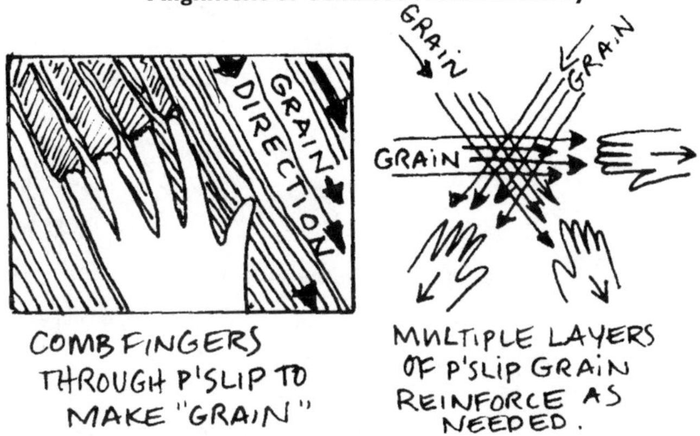

Control "grain" in paperclay slurry when it's fresh poured or at a smear or paste consistency. Let each fresh "layer" set up before covering it with a new layer. Build up multiple criss-cross fiber alignment layers when 3-ply lamination or extra reinforcement is needed.

Slip Cast or Press Mold

Can I cast paper clays in plaster molds?

The studio-made oatmeal style form of P'Slip you make in this book doesn't pour in ribbons like a traditional casting slip. Even so, smooth and exact surface detail from plaster molds results. Pour or smear P'Slip into an open mold, as in the photo on page 67. After several minutes, scrape off the excess overflow at the edge. If you prefer, roll the excess trim inward from the edge, and press it in, until it serves as double thick liner coil at the periphery of the cast image. Use a soft rubber rib tool, or your fingers. Do not let the mix dry out completely inside a plaster mold, or it will be difficult to release. It is easy, however, to release paper clay from a mold before it dries. Keep in mind that P'Slip sticks instantly to biscuit fired clay molds. For this reason I don't use clay molds. However, an artist reported that a single layer of tissue laid in the biscuit clay mold before a pour of P'Slip protected her P'Slip casts from sticking, but she lost the surface detail.

Find more detail on molds in the next chapter. It is easy to press and release wads, coils or slabs of P'Clay into dry rubber, clay, or plaster molds same as I would with traditional clay. As an artist, I see molds as a point of departure, not by any means a final result.

Slip Casting Prepared P'Slip® pours in and out of the opening in a normal ribbon from conventional multiple part slip cast molds and is a great convenience. Have durable, quick set castings, that travel well, and, can be repaired, if need be. I wonder how much longer it will take until people realize this idea works so well. P'Clay/P'Slip® licensed manufacturers are ready to make pourable kind of Casting P'Slip® blends up for you, as a custom request in the meantime.

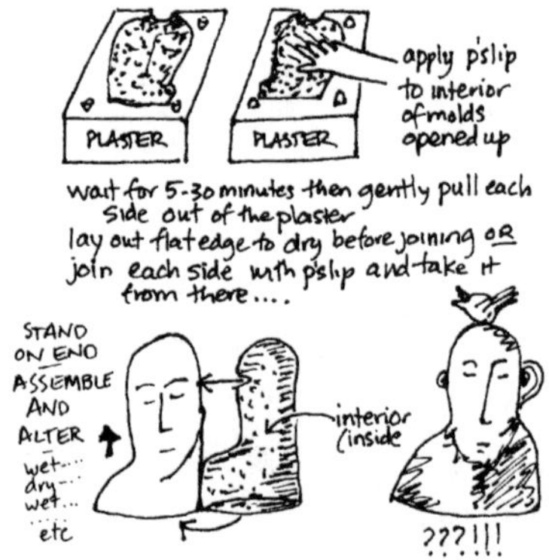

Chapter three

Large Scale Sculpture

3

Sculpture Revisited

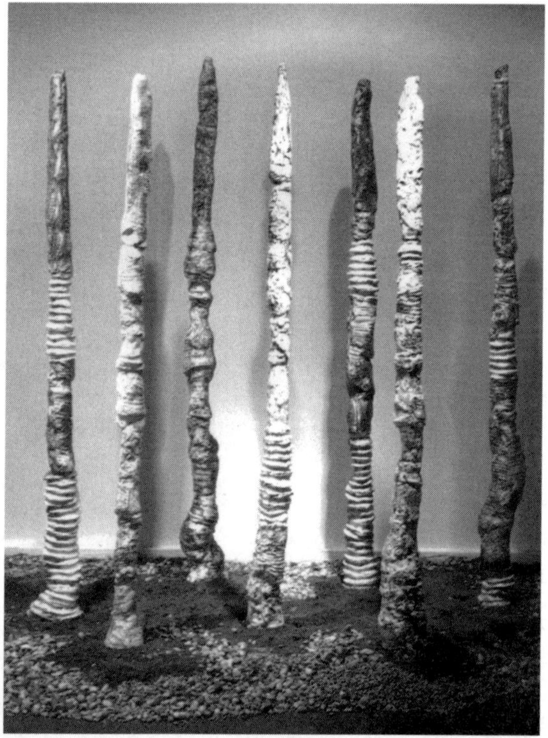

Fig. 36: Forms by Jenny Mulcahy, Australia

Are paper clays appropriate for scale-up to life size?

Complex assembled ceramic forms with colorful glaze are likely to survive not just the ordeal of construction and kiln fire but thereafter through time as a cultural record. They are therefore, worth the attempt. The totally dried state of a paperclay is available to us like never possible before.

Materials less vulnerable than clay have been preferred for large scale sculpture but each has technical limits to work around. Traditional sculpture clay, with non plastic stabilizers like grog in it, restricted us to work periods at leatherhard states of dryness. Oil base clay, like plasticine, gave us near perpetual plastic modeling but requires a wood or metal armature to support it. Polymer based clays can be modeled, but not fired. Plaster is stable and allows crisp detail and definition with clean machined smooth edges without a kiln like the classics seen on page 38. Wire net, wood, or foams are the typical armature support. Each sculpture medium has it's pro and con. In comparison, the discipline of traditional ceramic sculpture, even though it can mimic any material when finished, was frustrating to master. Paperclay ceramic when mastered, more than traditional clay, includes some of the best technical benefits of other sculpture materials just mentioned all in one.

In addition to modeling, there are infinite chances to mix and match parts that are bone hard and dry with soft. Intermittent drying between work periods allows the paperclay itself to serve as its own armature support.

Whether you add, or subtract, build up with thin walls, or carve down from thick chunks, whether your approach is conservative, or cutting edge, your best intention can be served. Large scale paperclay proves to have its own set of rules.

Issues irrelevant to small scale paper clay (and all clays) must be reckoned with upon scale up. Planning or reinforcing a base that can support the weight what is above matters. The internal frame and bracing and must be considered before the form is fired or if it is to be non-fired. Base weight, shrinkage, and balance, all factor in. Pay attention to the joins that will be weight bearing.

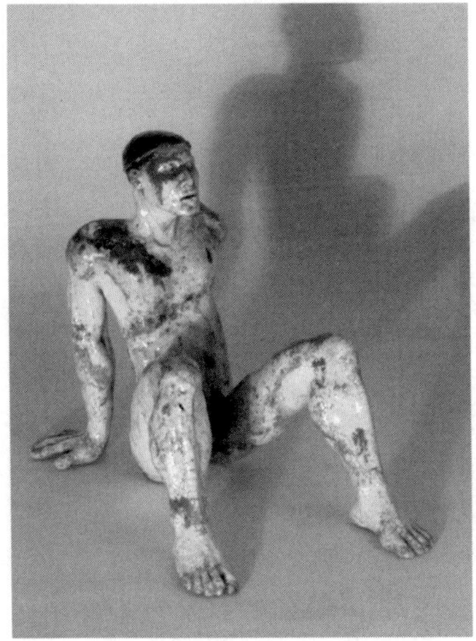

"Swimmer" by Carmen Lang, Mexico, Raku. (Ht. about 35")

Dimension of the available kiln, doorways, platforms, transport vehicles, shelving, and more, may become part of the plan. By the time a work stands at 48" or more, there are a few new rules and changes from tradition to know in order to have full freedom with it.

For life sized sculpture, should I add more pulp to the base clays than normal?

Yes. Add as much pulp to the base recipe as you can tolerate. A "VOLUME" (not weight) of 35-45% pulp is better to add, for large scale. When impractical, or too late, to mix a new high pulp batch, at least add extra pulp to the sealant/adhesive P'Slip you use to make joins. Mix-it-yourself artists find a whole chapter on balancing the pulp to clay ratio. My clay recipes in the appendix could be a guide. Please be sure to test fire first, since regional clays and pulps do vary.

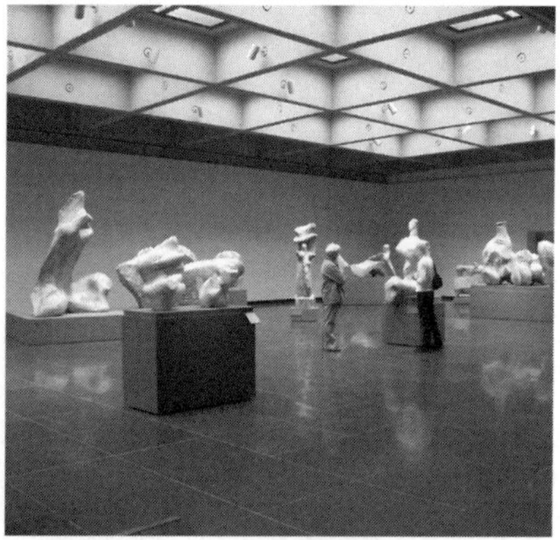

Fig. 38A: ***Original Plaster Models*** *used for bronze public sculpture by Henry Moore (1898-1986) to the left at the Art Museum of Ontario, in Toronto, Canada. Unlike the heavy plaster over wire mesh construction that Moore used here, durable models at this scale could be built and assembled at bone dry relatively quickly in paperclay ceramic. Moreover, the result could also be fired, glazed, and be much lighter weight.*

Fig. 38B: ***Balance:*** *Author with group of works that were both cast and handbuilt.*

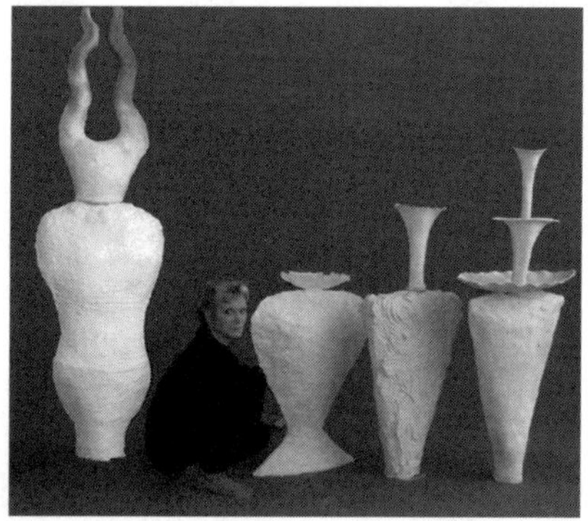

Grog and sand used to be among the only correctional additives to traditional sculpture clay for a leather hard and firing form stability. There is little or no reason to put these stabilizers and fillers in a paper clay. To avoid a rough texture, and get a super-smooth perfect surface to carve on, omit grog and/or sand entirely. Paper clays for raku need no grog or sand either.

Could I still get granular paper clay body burnout textures?

If you want to keep the texture of gritty clay as part of your style and aesthetic, try to cut it by half or even 3/4 in your base recipe. An alternative way to build in 'ultra texture,' and keep the fired weight to the minimum, is to add some granular burnout material such as perlite to paper clay instead

---

Fig. 39: ***Advance Planning for Big Molds:*** *I tacked "cutouts" of plastic bags (or paper) to the wall in the design phase for plaster molds. Later I would put the cutout shape flat on the floor for a guide edge to pile wet sand up on as in page 63, preparing for a plaster mold over top the sand. I could have used styrofoam or other material but the sand was the simplest to dispose of, affordable, efficient, and non toxic.*

Sandcast Plaster Molds *allowed fast drying production of dozens of ready textured bone dry paperclay "shells" to start the shapes shown on page 38 and 51. In a week or so I had 12 standing assembled and dried hollow forms ready to work and alter the surfaces at scale. Forms at bone dry were stable, lightweight, hollow, and surprisingly durable. The texture was an ideal grip for fresh layers, contours, or surface finishes.*

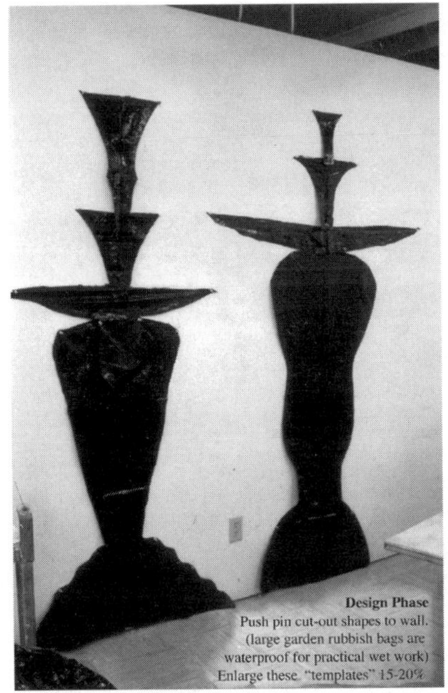

Design Phase
Push pin cut-out shapes to wall.
(large garden rubbish bags are waterproof for practical wet work)
Enlarge these "templates" 15-20%

of grog. A fired surface that attracts interest and attention is the "mystery rock" coral sponge effect you can get with combinations of pulp plus burnout material. Whatever you choose to add or omit, if you let the sum of the perlite/pulp total more than the clay, you risk a "crumbly" fired result rather than a solid form you intended. The same goes for total volume proportion of grog/sand/pulp combination. The more non clay "junk" added to the clay, the "shorter" and less plastic it is to model with.

How is the "shrinkage" of natural paper clay a "loyal friend?"

Count on large scale paperclay to cycle between move and pause, wake and sleep, contract and expand, at least twice over time before the project is finished. The more I tested, I saw how predictable the movements are. To review:

Movement One: Wet to Dry.

Paperclay forms contract as water evaporates. As the assembly shrinks from leatherhard

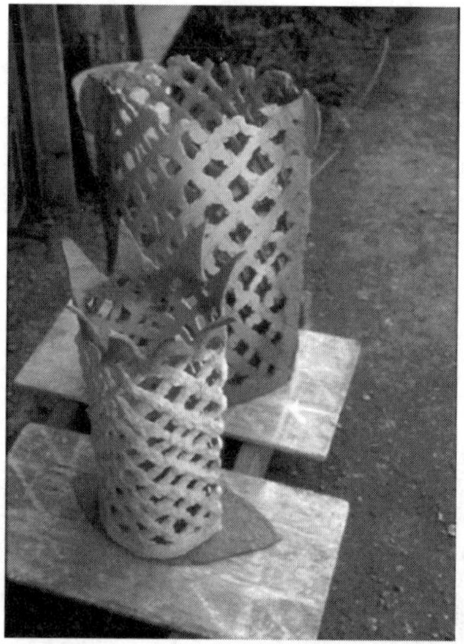

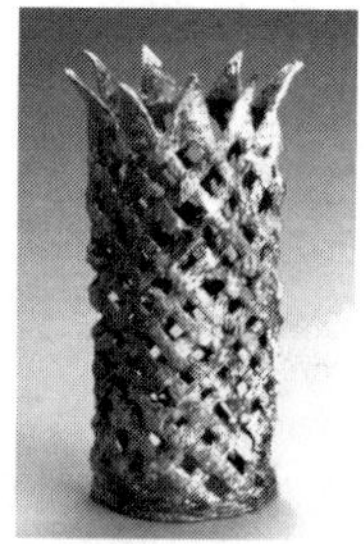

*Fig. 40A: **Lattice:** I dribbled P'Slip in lines across the flat plaster slab to make a interwoven open lattice. After the "lattice" set up enough to handle, I stood it on end for wet on dry assembly. Intermittent work periods yielded results to right.*

*Fig. 40B: **"Crown Mind as the Basket Case"** by author, 24 in. One fire to cone 6, glazed in bright color.*

to dry state in sun, open air or forced heat, well done joins and seams will either snug tighter together maybe move apart. Gain control which direction they go ahead of time by having curled the parts inward or outward a little more than you need at the leather stage before the join as will be explained in detail later. Leather hard paper clay is still "active" and shrinking in motion however slow. As such, to assemble at leather hard can interfere with the natural drying path of big clay slab. Wait to assemble till big sheets have quit moving and are totally dry.

The Pause Stage: Totally Air Dried

Shrinkage and movement rest. Did your shape survive this stress? If parts opened up to cracks, or are too thin you get to fix, change, reinforce them in peace. Assembly of big shapes, "paused" at bone dry, are far easier to control, and less risky to repair. See the photos on page 51. The course of construction continues until the appearance of the sculpture satisfies in every detail. So what if the paper clay sculpture contracts and expands slightly during re-wetting drying alterations and assembly of parts? The artist

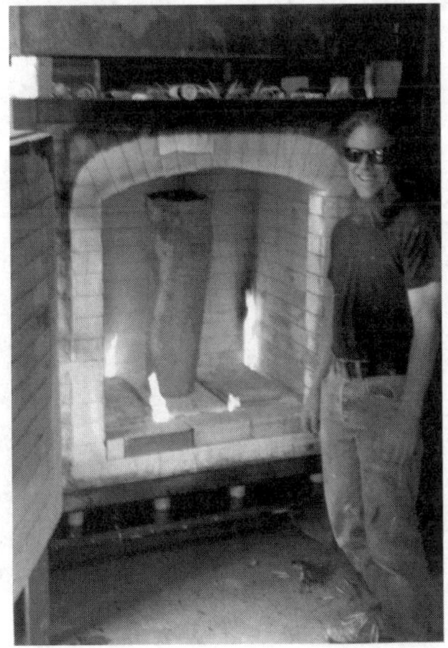

Fig. 41: ***Extreme "Toasting."*** *Force dry joins to set them if desired. Open kiln door keeps temperature below boiling point of water. If not enough pulp in your recipe, cracks in "join" will soon appear. You would still have plenty of time to reinforce and repair before the actual firing. This form by author dried intact in about 2 hours. Later, author's work was single fired to cone 6. Featured in photo Jon Williams and his kiln.*

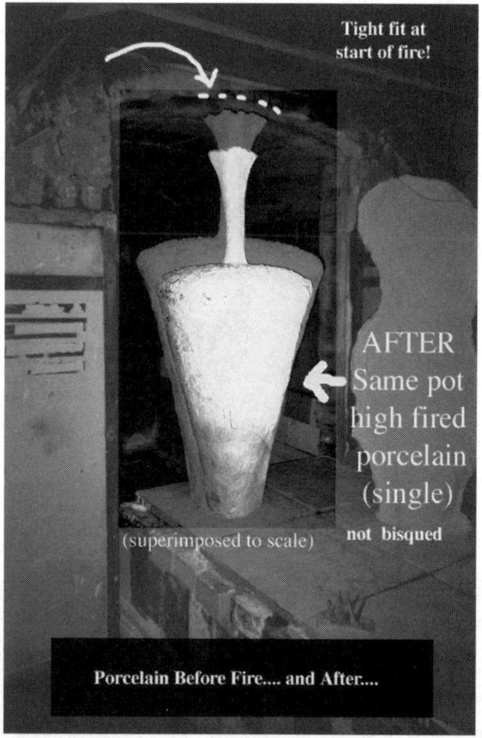

gets to switch between moisture states as the assembly occurs. By the time you finish, big structures should expand and contract without cracking.

Movement Two: The Fire. Behind the kiln door in the heat and flame the form changes to durable ceramic. Dare not interfere with hands and tools then. The moment of truth and final trial of your sculpture occurs.

If you observe closely, stress of open air shrinkage (from wet to bone dry)

Fig. 42: ***Make the most of natural shrinkage in fire****. Contraction and expansion of the forms and joins in wet to dry cycles before fire is a pre-flight test for changes in fire. Plan ahead for the natural "****shrink tight effect****" on seams, joins, and internal cross bracing. Superimposed, we see exactly how porcelain paperclay shrunk from a start height of 4 feet. Other base clays would shrink much less. A slight change in sculpture size was not as important as the benefit of having creative control, lighter finish weight, translucency if I wanted, plus durability and colors of the end result through time.*

mimics and predicts the path of future shrinkage in the fire.

To get a preview of how your sculpture will move in the kiln, simulate a similar situation in the first drying period. Resist the urge to "baby" works dry like you must do with traditional clay. Don't cover them. Slow drying is counter-productive for paper clay because the traditional procedure fails to stress the joins enough for the maker to assess the need for repair or reinforcement with any accuracy. Give them sun, open air, or a warmth but not above the boiling point of water so steam does not build up and has time to escape. Maybe force green ware to dry in or near a hot kiln.

Some paper clay mixtures developed stress cracks in tight spots at bone dry, can I fix them?

Yes. The root cause of the stress crack showing up at bone dried is typically not enough pulp. Add more pulp in the next batch to stop. Even so, most of the stress cracks (in lower pulp bodies) can be healed. The exact amount of pulp to add to stop the show of drying cracks can vary slightly with the type of base clay used. The actual percentage you settle on depends on variables of local pulp and regional clays impossible to predict with further accuracy than this. To remedy, meantime, I just stir in a n extra handful of wet pulp into my adhesive P'Slip, and I even make up a small amount of 'high pulp' soft putty. High pulp P'Clays have affinity with lower pulp P'Clays so seals and repair between them should hold up well, as was explained in reinforcements on pages 32-33.

Work Sessions over Bone Dry

Are the seal joins in bone dry better or stronger than in leather hard? When should I use the scoring method of preparing the surface?
The majority of joins at bone dry will be as strong or stronger than those attempted at leatherhard. Depending on the shapes joined, and the care taken by the sculptor, water in the P'Slip "thick oatmeal" will be absorbed and sucked down in the "thirsty" surface of the bone dry part. The tip ends of each wet fiber (cellulose) respond to simple water osmosis. Dry pores at the bone dry surface "suck" fibers in. But, fiber ends are "caught" as they extend down.They stiffen in the process of evaporation and dispersion of water. The "grip" between dry and wet resembles a "stop-action" fluid version of the fabric fastener tape "Velcro" that snags shut. Chapter 5 explains this in extreme detail.

The whole joint or work area undergoes a shrinkage and expansion process that is mediated by the presence of the hollow tubular cellulose fibers that wick water inside, between, around, and through the clay. As a precaution for high load joints, pre-score, re-wet, and rough up contact surfaces for maximum adhesion. A high load structural join must be secure enough to carry weight, load, or stress, after fire and finish.

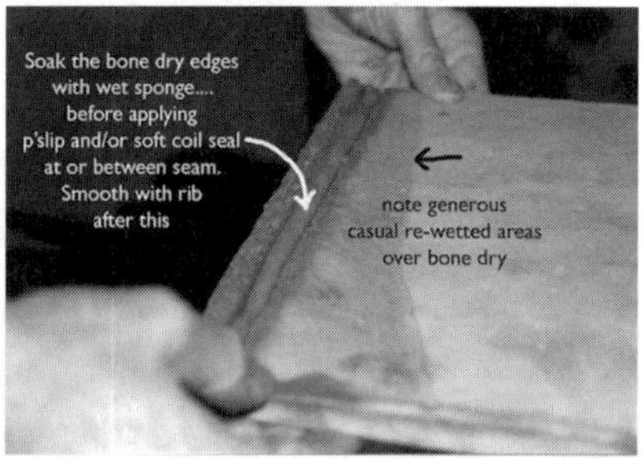

Fig. 44: ***Flat Box Construction****: Assemble flat slab sections* ***at bone dry*** *after they have stopped shrinking. They can be re-wet with a damp sponge in areas that you want or need as seen to left.*
If paperclay tiles didn't warp by the time they dried, they are likely to stay flat in fire. Cause of warp during the fire could come from either, over fire, over working/wetting them, or not placing them in a good place in a kiln. Big sheets of 0.05-3" thick paperclay can be fired flat, bridged over kiln shelves, sometimes over a trace of sand also.

Join between bone with soft is usually better that same join at would be leatherhard. If you assemble between leatherhard parts, a deep score procedure is a must, paper clay or not. Leatherhard stage paper clay pores are too "full" of water, and not dried out enough, to induce this "secret snag Velcro" osmosis benefit with bone dry explained earlier.

Most fully air-dried shapes stay put through the rest of the construction process. Most do not move or warp, unless over-fired. The presence of paper fiber stabilizes a flat tile shape, if you stay mindful of handling from the start until bone dry as in the diagram on page 47. A common error is to move and handle big leather hard (still shrinking) paper clay sheets and expect them to stay "put" for the reasons explained. Exception: if you have a bone dry thin walled slab and you dip soak it wet again, it will "curve" just a little in case you want or need flex. This feature, when needed, is a plus.

Which carry-over work habits from conventional clay practice are worth letting go of?

Many procedures for traditional clay do not carry over well to paper clay. Many are counterproductive. It took me more than a few years to "unlearn" twenty years plus of established habit, and defy hard learned technical limits. The effort was worth it. As I lost the old work habits, I gained in freedom. The three best questions I asked myself were:

Old Habit 1: ***Why "baby" clay forms with soaking wet towels and under wraps of plastic between work sessions?***
This great idea for traditional clay stopped me from taking full advantage of the bone dried states in paperclay as explained. The interior of my paperclay would never have chance to dry fully before new layers seal in moisture all the more. The bigger the project the worse the problem of trapped moisture gets. It can take months for the interior to get dried enough to fire if a traditional method like this is used.

Old Habit 2: ***Why bisque everything before glaze?***

Paper clay, at bone dry, is nearly the same water absorbency as a bisque. Work can be dipped in glaze bone dry and still hold its shape long enough for evaporation and uniform glaze adhesion to occur. Bisque fire used to be the <u>only</u> way to make conventional clay absorb enough water from the glaze to cause a uniform deposit of glaze on the surface without losing its shape. Single fires save time and fuel cost. I bisque to cone 04 as a practice.

Old Habit 3. ***Why assemble parts only at the leatherhard stage?***
As explained, most pre-assembled large scale leatherhard structures are not immune from movement and warp compared to their equivalents assembled at bone dry. Maintain better control of movement in the final result and get more chances to change and test for secure joins before its too late.

Why plan some work sessions for the bone dry state and avoid inner metal armatures?
Intermittent work sessions on, or over, the bone dry structure give the sculptor a degree of efficient control over the final outcome impossible to gain by other means. Most cut, trim and section procedures are more reliable then. Pre-shrunk and fully

bone hard assembly parts are more stable.

Wire or mesh armatures rarely serve a practical function. Recent aesthetic advance in fired paper clay by the "chicken wire school" is worth seeing, and is discussed further in Chapter 7. Bone dry paper clay will support weight just as well, or better than wire metals. Most joins bond right away, and are strong enough to be tested a few minutes later. Practical advantages like these reduce risk of fracture, and free an artist from need to weld metal or to endure further technical distraction from aesthetic concern.

How can I be sure my seams and joins will survive the fire? What is the "pre-bend" system?

The "pre-bend" technique insures a super secure join between very large slabs, coils or handles. To illustrate, an example with slab construction follows.

Cut two identical soft large slab shapes with a needle tool. Place each in separate but identical slump plaster molds. Bend edges of each soft side gently "in" a few inches "further

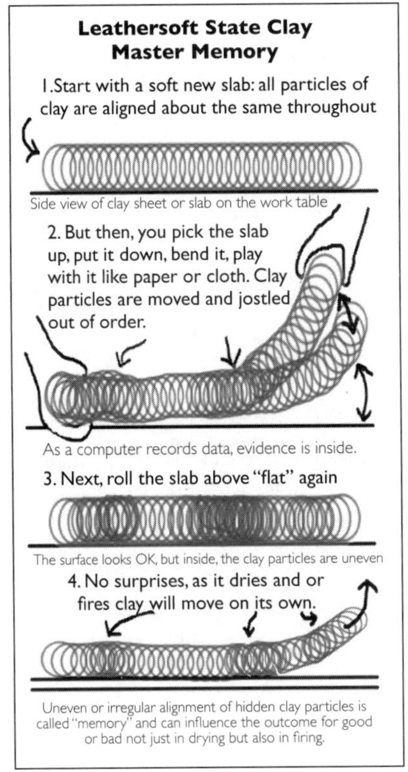

Fig. 47: ***Clay Follows Your Lead.*** *The bigger scale the clay is the more noticeable movement seems during drying or firing. As potters can control teapot spouts that move a bit "by themselves" during firing, so hand builders can control the direction of big slab torque in firing also. Handle soft slabs mindfully. The clay "remembers" the sequence and intensity of your handling directions in linear order.*

than I actually intend" as soon I can handle the soft slab gently without fingerprinting the surface. Then, I let each "shell shape" air dry in the approximate true curve I want. No one can see on the "outside" the 'secret suggestion' I made to the clay particles on the "inside." Study the diagram on the previous page, to better understand and control what happens 'inside' the big soft paper clay slabs as there is a simple logic to them. Adhere the two bone dry forms end to end with a seal of soft paper clay and P'Slip adhesive between them. When the seam dries without a crack, I know I added enough pulp to my clay for the size of the project. If not, a few surface cracks will show. I fill them in. I may add some extra pulp to the P'Slip oatmeal to help. Next big batch, I fine-tune the proportion of pulp I prefer with the amount I need for the challenge before me. In general the bigger the work, the more pulp. More information on adaptations for sculpture base clays is given later on this chapter.

During the stress of high fire, big works move but where else can they go but in the very same direction "bent or curled " earlier when in the soft state? Under stress, the form tends to shift and move in a direction of least resistance that will be mediated by natural force of gravity. Suppose the edges of two big curling (i.e. pre-stressed) slabs meet with resistance at the seam line, will they stop there? Not necessarily. In both phase one and phase two of shrinkage, the edges squeeze tight against each other at the join seam like a clamshell! All things being equal, if I were to over-fire such a seal, the walls collapse before the seams would open. I've tested this many times with a variety of traditional and paper bearing porcelain with very thin walls. If I use the same method, but orient slab or coils in reverse, expect seams and slabs to warp "open" like magic.

For the maker who desires to master the most difficult and unforgiving of clays such as porcelain, and porcelain paper clay on a large scale, this expert technique is my key to great joins, confidence, and a seamless result.

Can I use power or hand saws and drills on big bone dry or leather forms?

If I cut ***after*** the air set occurs, match-up between reinforced sections is quite stable and less likely to warp. I cut bone-dry paper clay apart with any kind of power or hand saw. Through thick dense areas, it may make sense to "pre- score" the potential cut line(s) in advance. Just before the wet clay stiffens, I scribe a "guide line with a needle tool. I leave approximately 0.25 cm of the clay line intact. At bone hard, the scribed line is a ready made "guide" for the saw blade. If my shape permits, I snap sections or tiles apart at bone dry. Straight score lines lend well to the snap-apart method on page 26.

For clean machine or power tool cuts in some high fiber clays and slabs, make a super sharp blade cut through a temporary additional layer of cloth or masking adhesive tape. It may help to sketch the intended saw path on the tape surface with a clear dark marker before you begin to cut. Remove the tape after.

In some situations, super crisp machine cuts are best done to a "sinter" rather than raw piece. Sinter fire method will be discussed in more detail in the section on carving down ultra thick chunks of paper clay coming up.

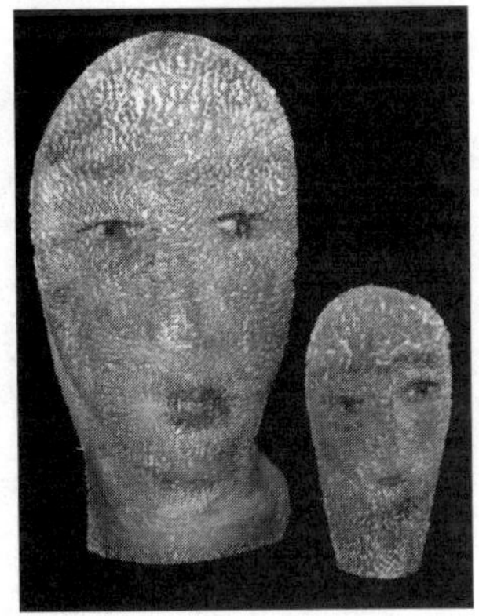

Fig. 49: "Extra Terrestrials" by Author, 18 in. and 7.5 in. freestanding. Glaze and clay fired surface texture for paperclay are detailed in my second book "Paper Clay."

When my work gets bigger than the kiln? What are some good ways of determining the best cut lines?

To fit figurative paper clay sculpture in a kiln, it often makes sense to divide the form up into to several smaller shapes. Best "cut lines" will be most clear when the full form stands in space. I view work from near, far, above, below, and around all sides.

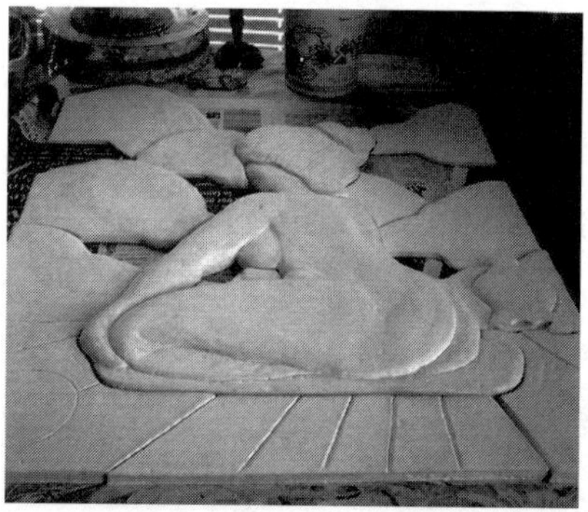

The better places for cut lines follow along natural curve crease lines that least interfere with smooth contours. Arbitrary horizontal straight "cut lines" interfere, and distract the eye from the art. Very few designs are well served by them. I use cut lines sparingly.

How can I plan so the "curvy" sections will stand securely in the kiln for the fire?

For many, the right "cuts" will be a curve and not a straight line. Yet, sections likely won't free-stand and balance on their own in the kiln over a curve. To temporarily balance the section during fire, I may prop it with a soft firebrick. I may improvise a bone dry "nest" or "scaffold" out of a large coil(s) of spare paper clay, or even a big bowl of vermiculite, or sand, as in the photo on page 52. I remove all such supports later after fire.

Fig. 50: ***Tile Layout and Fitting***
Work in Progress by Cynthia Dahlstrom. Cut between each tile as part of the design. Size and thickness of the different tiles parts can vary also.

What if my bone dry "parts" are too big to assemble on my own?

When bone dry parts are too big to tack together with two hands, tie belts of string, or masking tape, to hold the sections temporarily close together. As a preliminary to the full seal process, wad in balls of putty-soft paper clay to join parts of the at five or more key points, curves or corners along the proposed seam line as

Session 1:

Assemble dried paperclay shell castings

in stages with wet on dry methods.

Fig. 51A left: Session One and Two:

I balance two sand cast "shells" (see molds for them page 65) upright with a temporary band such as masking tape, then adjust the alignment between them.

The targets mark points where I tack B to A with soft balls of paperclay the size of large kiln wads. I let the balls dry out to secure the most stable connect possible between the two. At this stage, I leave big gaps open on non stress bearing seams. Bone dry "shells" are most stable as they are have shrunk down all the way. I avoid the leatherhard moisture state in big clay as it is in midst of active slow "motion" compared to the bone dry calm.

Fig. 51B right: Session Three:

Hours later, balls at target zones hardened solid and dried. Now big clay can't slip out of register. Structure is now stable and won't come apart while I cover over the bone dried balls and finish sealing seams together.

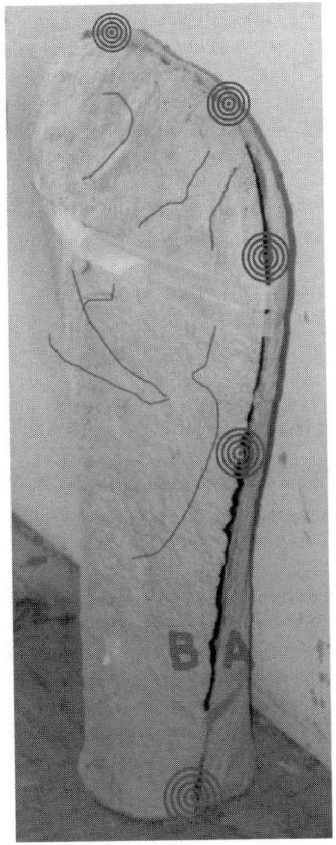

Session 2:

Targets show points where balls of soft paperclay were placed. Wait for the soft new p'clay balls joins to get really dry and stabilize the assembly.

Stand back,If you need to adjust the A to B alignment at its easier to undo or redo the wads at the points, ratherthan undo a whole filled in seam.

When structure is secure, fill the seam gaps with soft putty of p'clay and p'slip until smooth.

Session 3:

Seal Between the "Shells"

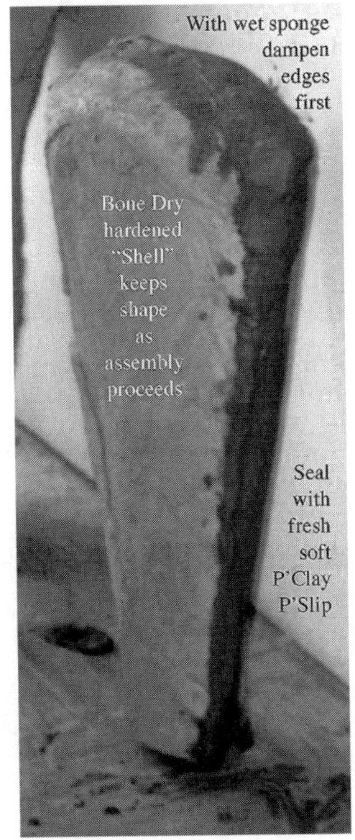

demonstrated in the photo chart on previous page. Adjust the balance and placement of these soft "flex-wads" until alignment between both sides is best. Paper clay "flex-wads" are strong enough to hold most big assemblies together long enough for fine tuning. Nudge the big assembly into final position. The "balls" will permit some play between the bone dry parts while you adjust them. Do not worry about filling big open gaps between the seams at this point. The flexing balls soon stiffen and turn hard at bone dry. The result is a very stable bone dry assembly structure to work over. At bone dry, remove the temporary belts of string or tape. By then, the new form may have tilted a bit. Slide shims of dry and soft wads of P'Clay under the base. This is often the easiest cure.

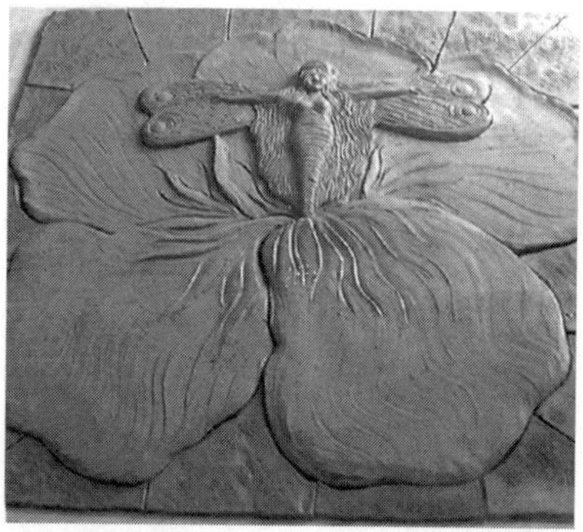

Fig. 52A: ***Bas-relief tile work*** *in early phases of design by Cynthia Dahlstom. Chances to carve and model up continue* ***far*** *beyond leather hard.*
Bone dry segments have nearly double green strength than conventional clay and are easy to transport. Note how tile cut lines harmonize with the image.

At this point, seal in seam gaps and model with fresh soft P'Clay putty coils or cut strips of soft/fresh P'Clay slab dipped in P'Slip as per the example shown in Fig. 51B. The structure of your assembled form stands strong, and is, more or less, unaffected by subsequent applications of weight,

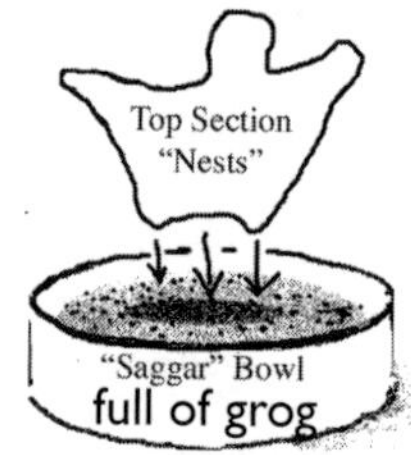

Fig. 52B: ***Support Sections During Kiln Fire:*** *A bowl full of grog, or some kinds of sand, can temporarily hold a section upright through kiln fire.*

friction, drilling, carving, interior and exterior contour refinements or reinforcements with P'Slip and P'Clay.

Any easy way to level out "wobbly" freestanding bone dry/bisque forms? Use scraps of dry paper clay and or soft coils or wads for shim. Just before loading in the kiln, double check for wobble, and smooth putty blend the new shims neatly in base.

A quick way to determine where exactly to shave off high areas on the bone dry base is as follows. Holding the base secure in both hands gently slide it back and forth a few inches in each direction. This will burnish the "contact points" a darker/lighter shine. Rest the piece on its side. Shave off the burnished areas with a metal rib or sharp knife. Repeat the rubbing process until you have three or four contact points that steady the balance of your bone dry form on a smooth level table top. A tripod of three wide contact points will be most stable.

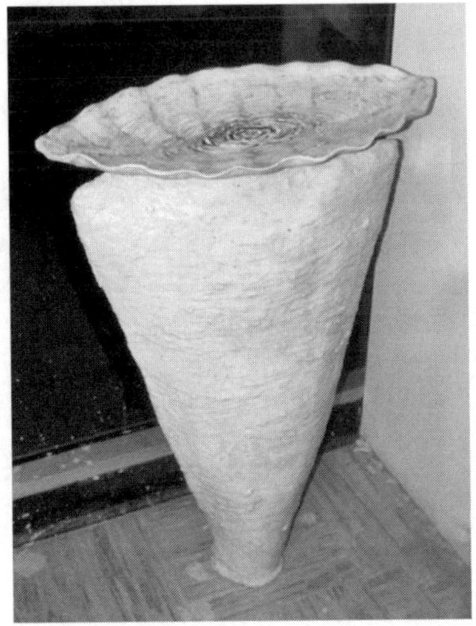

Fig. 53: Fountain Birdbath by Author. Hollow interior permits the water pump hookup. Hose leads water up to opening in center of the glazed bowl.

For large forms, is it better to trim, reinforce, and prepare for firing at bone dry state?

Yes. At bone dry inspection, I determine whether the new form has turned top heavy in the course of work periods. Also I check areas below "v" corners and any thin tube shapes. I thicken them up if they look weak usually by stuffing inside them with scrappettes, or I apply extra layers as described next.

In a four foot vertical span of a clay sheet standing on its edge, I prefer gentle taper up of the wall thickness to help support after fire. I build the form with even walls first. Then, at bone dry, I adhere a fresh soft slab, lattice, or coil, dipped in P'Slip, (soaked like "bandage strips,") to the interior weight bearing lower half to reinforce and/or thicken. Layers and or cross braces within stabilize the form. Unlike pottery, substantial base weight can reduce the chance of tip-over in the wind or by accident. Some remedy this at the time of installation by filling the hollow with heavy stones.

It may be a good idea to apply an extra soft coil along the rim of the bottom edge as needed. The interior "extra coil" is out of sight and lends extra support and stability, during transport and fire.

To trim and tidy up before fire, wipe or rub edges smooth with a damp sponge. I do not wait till after fire for this step. Soft "snips" turn razor sharp after the fire. Who wants sculptures that need "kid gloves" to handle? After fire, special tools to sand, file, or grind off the fired problem take time and effort to procure. Attention to detail before fire is the easiest and safest cure. For ultra crispy edges on no grog clays, consider sinter fire for the final sharpening and touch-up of carved detail with no interference from fiber.

Carve On Chunks like Stone or Plaster?

Any suggestions for carving on large chunks of solid or very dense thick paper clay?

Carving down a chunk of paper clay lends well to certain paper clay recipes or combinations thereof. Paper clay as a carving medium features some advantages to stone or plaster:

One: I get the chance to "invent" the ideal size, color(s), texture, density, hardness, fired weight, and composition of the "chunk" before I begin to carve saving a trip to the quarry. There would be less wear and tear on tools and blades too. I get to set the rough size at the soft easy stage.

Two: No trouble need be taken to hollow out the insides particularly if I put enough pulp in the base mix. I poke a decent opening in the underbelly my chunk of soft clay, and turn the chunk over to harden. When the chunk is dry, I start on the sculpture. Later when its time to install or fire the sculpture, I decide whether to fill in the hole(s) I made early on, or keep it. The opening underneath gives wiggle room for the thick walls of the structure to "expand and contract."

With stone or plaster you don't have as many choices of final finish and surface treatment as you do with paperclay. I force dry my blocks(s) for the "early warning benefit" of trouble-shooting movement in the kiln. If cracks show up, the cause and cure is same as explained earlier. Usually the batch needed more pulp. At this point, I decide whether to keep and carve through the fiber, or get rid of the fiber by means of a quick sinter fire.

I decide to carve in spite of the fiber, on bone dry, I re-wet the work areas

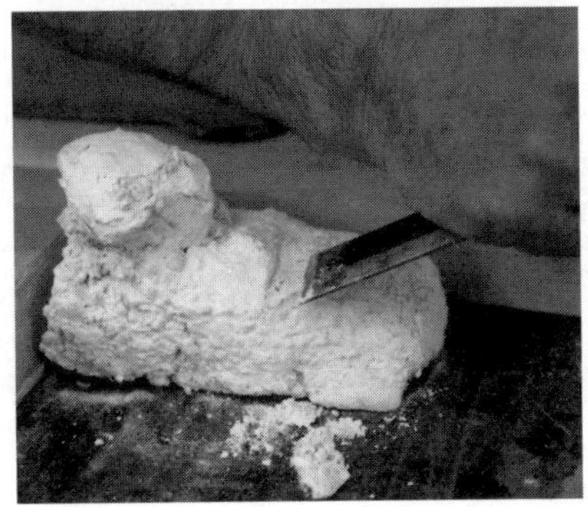

Fig. 55: ***Solid Block Like Stone or Wood:*** *Chip away on a totally dried block of porcelain with a hammer and chisel. If you make a mistake, just patch it up wet over dry. Let the patch dry totally hard and carry on.*

with a sponge as I go to help ease the resistance and re- soften the fiber a bit. I keep my tools sharp. Experienced sculptors have no problem with carving perfect detail on the bone dry, but those with less years of practice, may not yet have the knack, the skill, or the best tool blade, to get the effect they desire. Fortunately, it is easy to remove the fiber, and a pleasure to carve without it, on a ***sintered*** paper clay. Heat the chunk to sinter out the paper fiber. 570C (or 1000F) is hot enough to do the job and takes but a few hours. The result is a soft surface that resembles soapstone or soft plaster. Paper clay in this state has a feel all its own. The texture is smooth, and detail is impeccable, especially so, with a fine grained non grog, non sand, base recipe of paper clay. Power tools can be used with caution. In the event of error, on sinter or bisque, soak the affected area with water and rebuild fresh over top. If cracks develop I can repair most of them, as explained earlier.

I achieve any smooth or textured surface finish I can imagine by burnish or glaze. Mimic the appearance of almost any material your skill level permits. Then, seal a finish with either a permanent coat of colored glaze to fire gloss or matte, or not to fire and use a varnish, or paint or stain, etc. Stone and plaster and wood and most other sculpture media are limited in comparison.

Plan Ahead for Assembly and Installation

Should I plan ahead and build for easy install and de-install?

It makes sense in large scale, to plan before fire, or earlier for final installation. I plan for a generous interior hollow in the armatures to admit support tubes if, or when, I might someday want them. Holes drilled as last minute afterthought in bone dry paper clay will: ***a)*** shrink in diameter (if fired) and ***b)*** be limited to the diameter of the drill bit and torque power of the drill.

If it had been necessary to section the form so it could fit in a kiln, I reattach finished sections on site with a gasket of marine strength epoxy resin or silicone rubber. If flexible stability in wind or traffic is desired, I plan to mount a big work as a "sleeve" or "slip cover" over an upright semi-flexible plumbing PVC tube, pole or post. A semi-flexible tube, or post should be counter sunk down in the ground, or welded on a wide plate. In the event that the sculpture would ever be moved or de-installed, it may make sense to put a second sleeve of PVC plumbing tube inside my sculpture to

Simple Install and De-Install

Slide Assembled Sculpture over post.

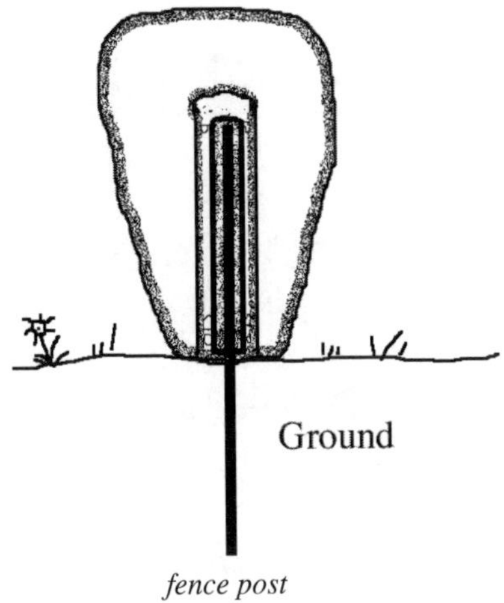

Cutaway Side View

Fig. 57, ***Install:*** *Plant big clay sculpture over a fence post. Consider prevailing winds, weather, and traffic in your placement plan. Sometimes, the fence post itself needs to have a little flexion. In case the sculpture is bumped by accident, a "flex" post absorbs shock instead of the ceramic. See page 58 for diagram of the interior assembly.*

make the "lift off" removal easy. Plan for this, by test fitting the sample right sized plastic inner tube loosely in the aperture hidden under your "armature" before fire. Allow some wiggle room when fitting, before fire, not just for shrinkage, but also for layers of adhesive.

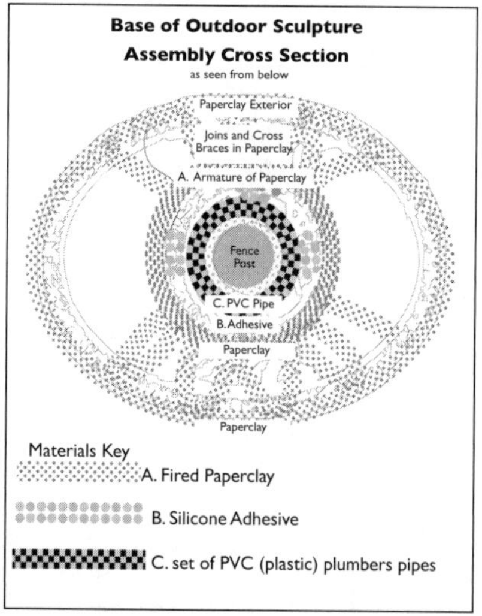

If the install is ***outdoors*** allow enough flexible adhesive (like silicone gel) to allow for expansion and contraction of all parts in extreme temperature. Avoid trapping rainwater/snow melt into "enclosed" pools or big pockets by careless use of adhesive too. If the available space fills to the brim and turns to ice, the ice expands. Rigid clay walls nearby the hidden insertion tube may not be strong enough to resist the stress of an hidden puddle of ice expanding. Both schools of precaution for freeze, frost, thaw "work." Either keep your paper clay unsealed, and open it to breathe at the bottom, as I do with success, or seal all parts off completely. Since base clays vary so much, I can offer you only increased understanding of the process. The higher pulp custom blends of P'Clay are proving well outdoors so far.

Fig. 58: ***Base for Big Sculpture:*** *Plan interior structure to serve* ***double duties:***

First: *For cross brace support to vulnerable or thin areas from inside add ultra light mix paperclay putty and tubes (part A in sketch to left) If you kiln fire, this is a way to control and even stop slab movement for high fired porcelain, or the like.*

Second: *For installing or de-installing as seen on page 57, measure the diameter of the paperclay armature tube (part A) to be wide enough (after fire) to receive a set of two (part C) of hard plastic plumbers PVC pipe or equivalent. Thus, after gluing pipe inside, the interior finished assembly can slide smoothly up and over a fence post.*

Finishes and or Glazes

Any other suggestions for success in large scale firing?

To get the permanence, look, and feel of ceramic clay and/or glaze, kiln fire is required. The reward is a permanent aesthetic document built for endurance in time. The fired weight of remainder clay is less than the average traditional clay as well. There is no need for any metal or mesh armature. Translucent quality of high fire porcelain is possible on a large scale. Most all fired paper clays prove outdoor and weatherproof.

The firing process enhances surfaces like paints can never quite do. Today, there are ready-made reliable ceramic glazes that minimize surprise because "what glaze looks like before the fire is NOT necessarily "what you get" after. It used to take years of experience to get good glazes from scratch.

Both traditional and paper clays when fired resemble stone. Extreme or sharp shock is their greatest vulnerability, same as stone.

Few kilns fire perfectly even temperature from top to bottom. Hot spots and temperature variance of several cones- 20 - 50 degrees are normal, no matter what the fuel. Freestanding forms larger than one meter often span the full limit of the kiln.

A thin clay wall carrying too much "load" above it is subject to the pull of gravity over time at high temperatures. The danger of slump or collapse increases as you approach the melting point of the base clay. Thin walled porcelains are most vulnerable, followed by stoneware so check them ahead. At bone dry, reinforce the walls from the inside and behind out of sight.

Be sure you have found the best firing temperature for the mix too. If you want a bisque fire go to cone 03 or 04. High fire stoneware or porcelain paper clay bisque can be soft, and even crumbly at cone 08.

As a precaution in big porcelain, lower the temperature to about cone 8. Hot spots of cone 10 or more are likely in big kilns no matter what the cone near the peep hole says. too. As you attain expert understanding of porcelain variables like structural mechanics for your specific shape, form of porcelain, skill level, and kiln, you will know exactly how hot, how tall or how wide, how thick or thin you can go. The master of the fire understands all phases between solid and fluid in large porcelains and the best moment to cut off the fuel.

Another possibility is to prepare a controlled melt design. For example, set two thin porcelain shapes to "drape down" or "partially melt in" upon one another. Stop the fire before total collapse occurs. No human hand can sculpt the natural curves that result if you time the "turn off" right.

Alternatives to Kiln Fire

What are my options for air set-non-fire paper clay sculpture?
Choices for final finish of my bone dry, not fired, form exist with paper clays at room temperature. It may be that, once I build it, a kiln the right size becomes available years later. Then, I wait. The piece will keep indefinitely under shelter unless... I toss the sculpture into a swimming pool and don't fish it out right away. Then my form would slake down to muddy P'Slip. Hurricanes, backyard hose downs, and other water play by man, or by nature, will break down the surface.

For those who don't want to wait for kiln access, air set finish is a real possibility. Either way, you win. Air set green paper clay is far less brittle than the same form in fired ceramic. WYSIWYG, or "what you see is what you get" finish methods reduce risk of further change in size, color, shape, or weight. There is no size limit. Wax, paint, polyurethane, acrylic, and oil, all adhere well. Shine up is easy, by burnish or polish methods.

When you scale up with an air-set preference, do not overlook the good features of other plastic and semi-plastic modeling media. Compared to paper clay, a concrete, or ultra dense plaster, is quite heavy and requires an inner metal mesh armature to start on. So does the distinct medium of papier-mâché. Many variations of not-for-a-kiln lightweight materials, plasticine, plastics, waxes, and foams exist and may serve in combination, or as alternatives.

What's the difference between paper clay, papier-mâché, and hobby modeling clay?

Papier-mâché differs from paper clay in composition. Machés are composed of a majority paper pulp and white adhesive glues. A fraction of kaolin type clay is included in the mix for smoothing. The forms air set to harden, and the "glues" ensure that they do. If these are fired in a kiln, the entire structure crumbles to dust and ash.

Commercially available modeling materials take this a step further. Plastics, perfumes, bright colors, acrylics, oils, wax, precious metals, et. al., are introduced into sophisticated (and expensive) art clays. Examples include the air set hobby product "Creative Paper clay" used by doll-makers and jewelers, "Sculpy," "Play Dough," "Celluclay," and many other trademarked distinctive modeling products.

For ultra-lightweight temporary non-fire projects, blend your wood glue and pulp maché with ground recycled styro-foam pellets. If these ever get in a kiln or fire, beware of the toxic fumes! Plenty of good books exist about paper sculpture. That field has a long history that we, in paper clay ceramic, can learn and borrow from.

Paper Plaster Combinations

Disperse a modest amount of pulp to plaster mixtures to lend some strength to life size molds. Measure the proper volume of room temperature water for your batch and measure the plaster dry in a separate bucket as per the recipe and directions in back of this book. Disperse some "handfuls" of wet pulp to the measured amount of water and stir. Then, sift the plaster into the water. Usually, small "islands" show above the water line. Stir and mix as usual.

The more pulp dispersed in the measured water, the less "room" for plaster. The more leftover plaster you have, the lighter the weight of "pulp plaster" will be after the plaster sets up. While lighter weight is a clear advantage for a life size "shell" of plaster, too little plaster equals an airy "mold" too soft and crumbly to travel and store well. In the end, a little pulp helps, a lot of pulp hinders. Trudy Golley inspired me to try blending pulp in plaster.

Big Sand Cast Plaster Mold

Large scale sculptors like me who needed or wanted to have giant plaster molds for their paper clay soon found a practical easy method to prepare them. Build a hump or slump with wet sand over a board or door blanks treated with smooth water-resistant flat clean surfaces like Formica or its equivalent. Maybe use a flat template shape under the sand or coarse road grade snow gravel. Some templates I used were seen on page 39. When I piled up wet sand over the template I had a boundary limit and guideline. I could replicate the same edge with infinite contours too.

Use thickened plaster, this time, to cover the moist sand hump or open hole. After the plaster hardens, on a hump of wet sand, gently slide the new mold side ways a few inches or so. If I have a smooth base surface, the lip of plaster will release from contact with the surface, and the pile of sand underneath will slide too. Then, it's safe to pry the new mold up.

Embedded sand lends a good texture to the surface of the plaster. The presence of leftover embedded bits of gravel in the plaster shell did not stop absorbency of the plaster below over time. Drape slabs of paper clay

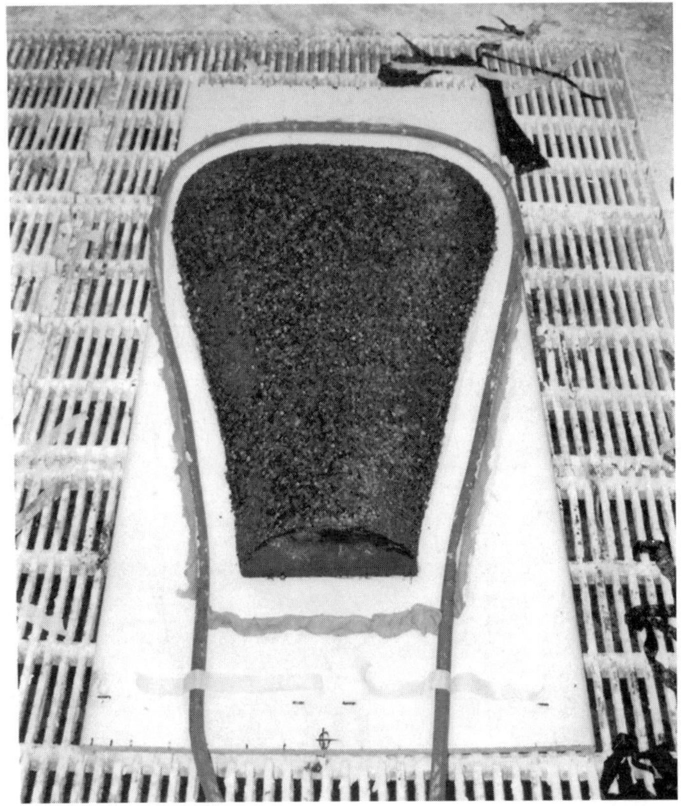

Fig. 63: ***Before the Plaster is Cast.*** *Prepare a hump of sand in advance. I "pat down" the wet coarse sand over top of a plastic template cut-out. Garden hose and seal clay coil served as a "cottle" or dam to keep the fluid plaster pour from leaking out. At time of plaster pour, the wall thickness of the plaster cover over the sand hump will be difficult to judge without some toothpick guides poked in sand at intervals that will stick up through.*

Direct Set Paper Clay Slabs or P'Slip In or Over Sand

into the plaster mold forms. Most paper clay shapes dry out evenly upon them. Most easily release at bone dry from the mold despite the sandy looking plaster surface. The rough texture imprinted on the surface of the paper clay form eases the process of assembly and alteration between multiple bone dry shells and shapes.

If I don't like the texture, but I do like the basic shape, I start to scrape, carve and sculpt whatever surface I prefer through the sand as soon as the plaster has set up and I released it from the sand pile. Etch deep lines, for example, like tatoos. When the mold itself is fully dry, after a week or so, be it.

Those new to plaster procedures may refer to the appendix, and/or other authors.

Set fresh made paper clay directly over or in shapes of sand or fine gravel instead. This is ideal for "one-off" shapes that you will not want to re-do. There are several easy choices. One decision will be whether to build a hump of wet sand or dig out an open hollow in a bucket, sand pit, or even, a beach!

If you build a hump of wet (sticky) sand, take time to pat down a smooth

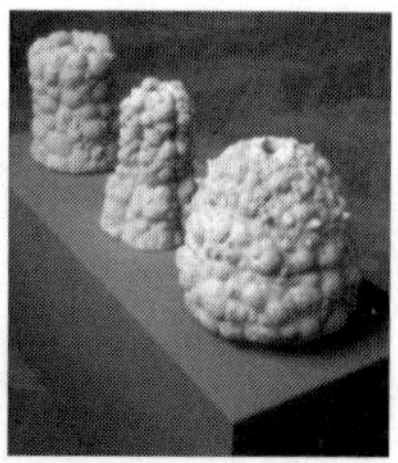

Fig. 64: ***Direct Sand Cast Form****s by Karen Hvsabo, Denmark*
Hvsabo mentioned that she and others at the Royal Academy of Art in Copenhagen, Denmark were casting paperclay slurries and slabs directly in sand to set up like in this picture. Her work triggered my imagination to adapt the process for big molds.

contour and keep the sand from drying out as you design by periodic water spray as needed.

To get a perfect shape at the bottom of the hump, it may help in advance to measure and cut out a template for the bottom in cardboard or plastic as seen earlier in the chapter. Then, pile up wet sand over top of the template and keep the guide edge in view at all times. With hump shapes, it can help to imagine what the shell cast of paper clay will look like if turned upside down, and/or inside out, after it is pulled up from the hump. Hump molds are a bit more technical than the hollow molds because you have to keep an eye on them from start to finish. The sand in the hump has to be soaked more often to keep it wet, too. Also, the shell of paper clay is best pulled off just before it is leatherhard.

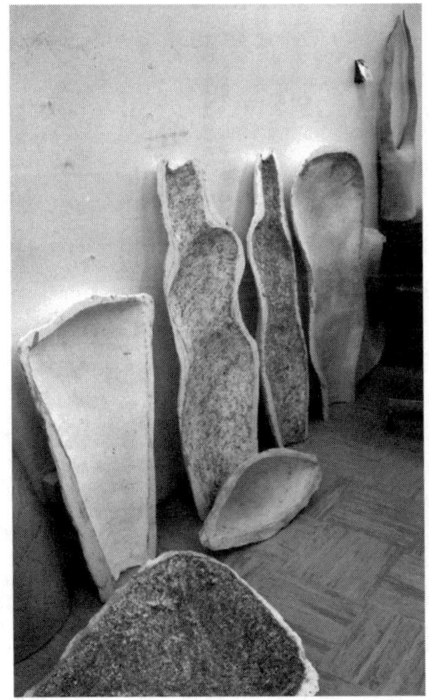

Fig. 65: ***Plaster Sand Cast Mold Shapes****: Lay one of these open and flat on the floor. Slump and or press a leather soft slab or slabs of P'Clay inside. To avoid sticking, if you poured P'Slip slurry directly in, do lift casting up at least once before it dries. Either way, let the whole leatherhard shell go bone dry with support of the mold. The paperclay takes the sand texture perfectly while the plaster still does it's drying job even under a rough sand surface. The few stray sand bits embedded on my P'Clay castings did not make a problem even at in high fire. The mold on the floor in this picture to right was pulled of the sand hump seen on page 63.*

The shell should be set with care so as not to stress or bend the "lip-edge." In time, the paper clay casting will finish shrinking and attain a bone dry state.

Slump sand shapes may not be as fussy as hump style shapes. The big paper clay sheet you set in a slump hole can, and probably should, stay undisturbed in the mold until bone dry. Pat, tap down, and smooth a good looking hole of wet sand in a bucket, sand box, or beach. Again, imagine the cast shape will be turned inside out and upside down in the end.

The only other decision is whether to cast thick oatmeal P'Slip "as is," or whether to make it into a soft drape slabs first. Press the slabs in, or over, the sand. Soft slab drape has many convenient advantages over direct pouring of P'Slip. One, is that the new shapes set up. and dry faster. Two, is the walls of the cast are automatically more uniform. The sacrifice is that the sandy surface texture may not pick up, and potential surface crinkles may have to be filled in later at bone dry. These distractions can always be corrected on a paper clay, of course. But some do not want to take the extra time, or may not have the patience, and enough skill to work the surface texture right.

The other choice is a direct pour of thick P'Slip. If you pour in a hollow, be prepared to scoop out the extra the pools in the bottom. Be prepared for a series of multiple pours. High humidity can increase the set up time by days. Pouring straight out of the bucket over a hump of sand is risky. It's likely the pressure from a heavy falling stream pour of P'Slip will dent the contour of the soft wet sand. Apply really thick P'Slip by handfuls, one by one, from the bottom up. Splatter or stipple methods may suit you also. Abundant and variegated textures result. The rest of the procedure for joins, fire and finish is as normal for paper clays.

What are some chances to improvise on beach or gravel cast forms?
Sand cast paper clay shapes can be free-form and playful indeed. Imagine a group of artists on a beach prepare sand humps and slumps. These serve as temporary nests for draped slabs of fresh paper clay in bright hot morning sun, with or without a gentle breeze. Assume the tide, or a rain storm, doesn't come in, the cast shapes dry to bone dry in a few hours, or even less if they are thin walled.

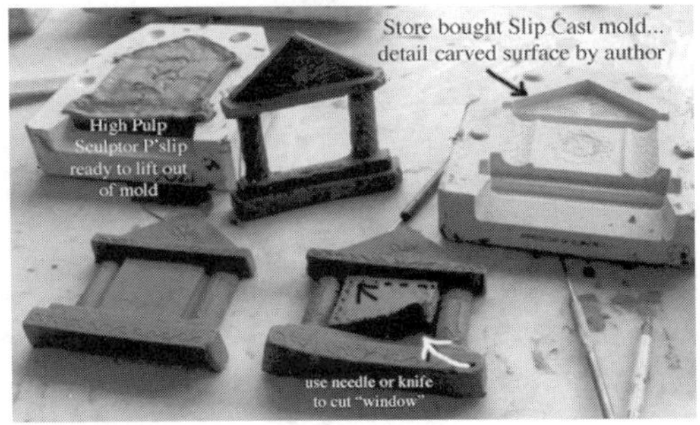

Fig. 67: ***Customize Commercial Plaster Molds.*** *With a sharp fettle tool, I carve surface detail in commercial slip molds with clay carving tools, then I clean off plaster powder remainder with water. After the soaking wet mold dries out, castings of paperclay release from it normally. Details on molds serve as a time saving point of departure for assembled sculpture creation not the end result they would need to be in a factory situation.*

Stand bone dry shells on end, balanced upon one another to amuse and please the eye. Good pairs can be joined together. An artist might model and contour over bone dry. Many ideas and combinations can be tried out as the afternoon passes by. Walk around, through, and perhaps, under the forms. Drag them around. Take them apart. Put some back together. How high could they stack? Collaborate. Some raw shapes become giant sand crayons. Nothing stays permanent until the artists get that "deep knowing" sense it looks right. Recycle or re-sculpt over shapes that don't make it. The "keepers" will be strong enough to carry and load in the back of your wagon, or truck, for firing, or further refinement. A beach bonfire that evening is one way to end the work period on a dramatic and social note. Ocean soaked beach timber is a ready and tempting fuel for the evening bonfire of the days best

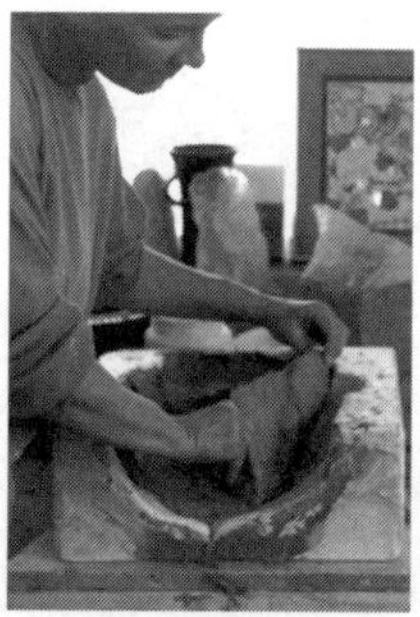

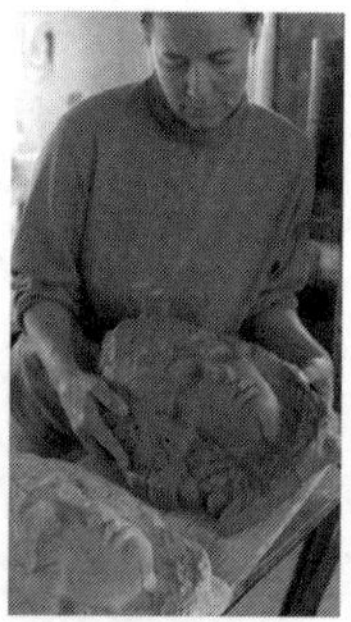

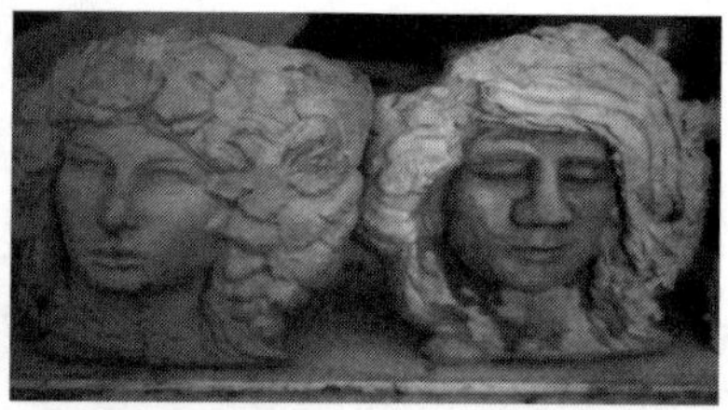

Fig. 68A (left): Sculptors "Face-lift:" *Ree Slocum lifts a leathersoft P'Slip casting of a generic "face" from a two part plaster press mold.*

Fig. 68B (middle): Twins and Multiples from a Single Mold: *Some castings from the mold in Fig 68A.*

Fig. 68C (right): "Trans Gender Study:" *A process of changing a "sister" to a "brother" is underway. Cheeks, eyes, jaw, brows, lips, and etc., are modeled "wet over dry" directly over her face. Infinite unique individuals could spring from the one source.*

work. Start the bonfire slowly in and around the bases of the works. Don't make the walls too thick. Obviously, a bonfire supplies direct and uneven heat stress to large structures. Consider tapering the width of some upper walls thinner so the bottom can be an slightly heavier anchor. Smaller sized handheld shapes are more portable and far easier for introductory beach fires. Just preheat them at the edge of the fire to dry them out after modeling. Turn them with a stick until you are satisfied each is hot and dry. Next, with a stick, gradually nudge them into the coals, and gently cover them in same. As night falls, fire light shines down the beach, and more wood is added. People gather round. Next morning, the tide will have come in and cleared the sand. In the ash of the fire pit, chances are extremely good to dig up, or see fired clay in shapes of wonder and beauty.

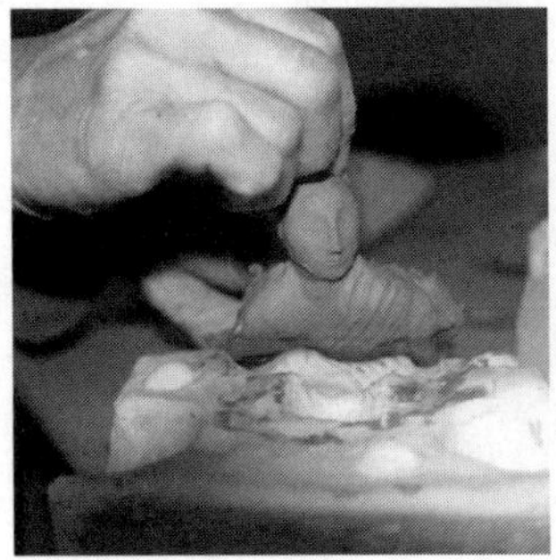

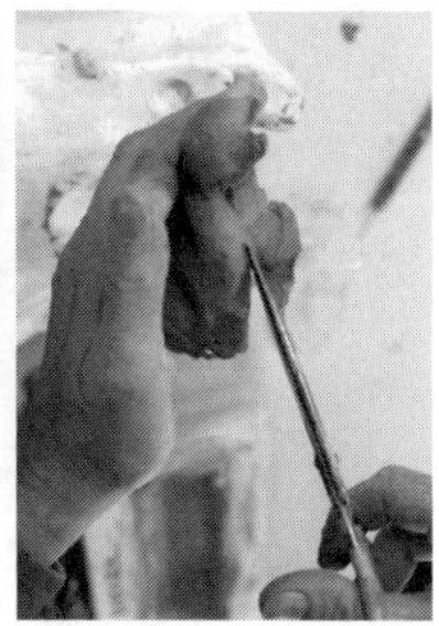

Fig. 69A (left): ***Handle Castings at Leathersoft State:*** *"I lift the figure up with the extra "tabs" of excess clay to help. This way I avoid disturbing crisp detail on a face.*

At bone dry, I select, join and assemble dried cast parts such as heads, hands, arms, feet, by mix and match to construct a sturdy assemblage.

Fig. 69B (right): It's possible to trim extra flap off a fresh "casting" with scissors or needle before I let the cast shape harden in the position I want. Re-define the undercuts and crisp detail in the cast face or form if desired. Stronger green and leathersoft strength allows this.

Improvise with Plaster Molds or Latex

Because of their strong green strength, paper clay slip castings or press molded forms are easily pulled out at leather stage. If you leave "extra" overflow during the pour as a clay "tab" to help start the job of release, so much the better. Cut the tab off after you release the cast. Notice that if thick P'Slip is used, no matter how much pulp is in it, the absorbent plaster sucks the fine particles to the surface and perfect castings result! If you use just P'Clay®, it should be very soft to get a good "print."

Trim or carve anytime after that. If you are casting a "face," please re-work the features so it comes to "life" again. If it's a mask, please "wake it up," open its eyes! Artists and students have no excuse for producing clone faces, our world already has plenty to go around. I consider all molds as a starting point and a shortcut tool... not the final. For example, a single mold can yield a set of five nearly identical castings of a mask or face in a day or so. But the artist works on each as an individual personality. Change the cheek and jaw bones, the expression in the eyes, which way they are looking, the hairdo, the lips, the nose... the race, the sex, and so on. Put small undercuts back in corners to add crisp contrast and highlight details of choice.

Another way to personalize your cast from mold work is to is to carve surface detail directly into a generic store bought plaster mold as was shown in photos on the previous page. The plasters used for most "slip cast designs" are soft enough to permit this.

Professionals may use latex-like rubber molds because latex offers light weight portability compared to plaster and chance for "undercuts." Just let the P'Clay **harden** all the way before peeling off the latex. Stephanie Snyder took latex casts of barnacle covered sea rocks and her paper clay castings gave a precise texture, an example of how latex might be used.

Chapter four

Potter's Report

4

Paper Clay and the Potter's Wheel?

No matter what form of P'Clay you choose, it has a distinct new texture and "feel" wheel, compared to what you might be used to.

If you want to try throwing, both Sculptor's or Potter's blend are OK. Your skill level and goals determine the better choice.

The "mix your own" paper clay, is not as easy to wedge and wheel throw, if it is too stiff. Be ready for copious slurry when you throw studio blend in comparison. To get the benefit of wet over dry, add enough paper in your studio mix.

The commercially prepared soft pre-wedged varieties of P'Clay® feel almost "normal" by comparison to the hand wedged studio mix. A potter typically trims edges of traditional clay before it dries out to bone hard.

Potter's blend is better for smaller works as trims up easily at leatherhard too, far more easily than Sculptor's. In other words Potter's blend will better meet the need of the more traditional pottery approach. Page 74 has more specifics on why this is so.

Beginners can learn to "center" with either type of prepared P'Clay just as well as with conventional. I noticed this when I taught introductory clay classes in Seattle. We used Sculptor's blend as the all purpose class clay since it can serve either throwing or handbuilding.

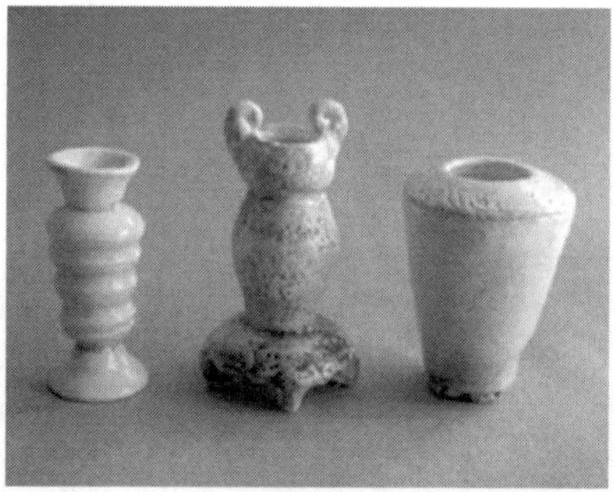

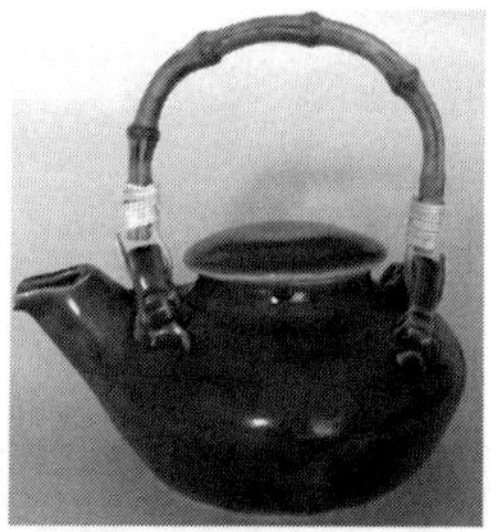

Handle It: Feet, and Complex Forms:
to Left: Wheel thrown and assembled bone dry with pulled handles by author with Sculptor's White Earthenware P'Clay® from Clay Art Center, Tacoma, WA USA. Fired cone 6.
To Right: Example of porcelain high fire (cone10) reduction teapot by author.

About Throwing with Sculptor's Blend P'Clay® on the Wheel

Wedge this clay at a minimum to avoid drying it out. Adept potters, who throw large and assembled parts, might choose the Sculptor's Blend for best green strength and versatility. I throw and wet trim "even" walls *before* sliding the pot off the wheel to dry out. Depending on the quality of the base clay, and the manufacturer of the P'Clay®, certain stoneware Sculptor's blends are easier to throw than others.

For general purpose handbuilding, tabletop, or bookshelf sculpture, the Sculptor's blend will be close, or just right. It contains a medium amount of paper.

For example, pots I made, shown in this chapter, are Sculptors P'Clay® from Mile Hi Pottery Supply of Denver. "Biz-Bod" was the base. I found it supreme to throw and fire, in high fire reduction, raku and oxidation kiln conditions. Thank you, Biz, for such a super base potter clay recipe.

If you plan to throw big life size sculpture or architectural sections, that are lighter weight, you may want to increase the amount of pulp in your studio made blend. My personal blends are included for your reference in this appendix.

All P'Clay® licensed manufacturers are prepared to mix and pug custom higher pulp sculpture bodies for you. If you ask, the manufacturer will consult with me personally to get your special base clay with high pulp pugged right.

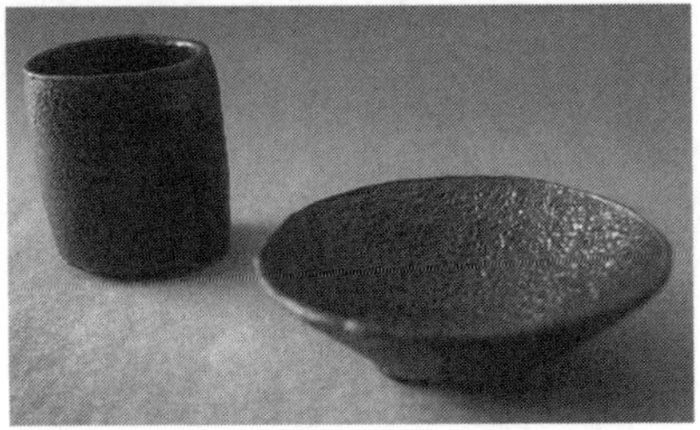

***Raku** by Author, wheel thrown with Mile-Hi, Denver Biz-Bod Sculptors P'Clay®*

About Potter's P'Clays

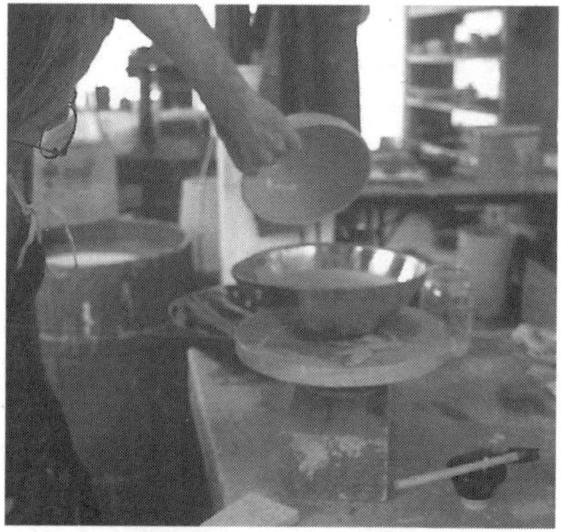

Dip Bone Dried Pot in Glaze: *Jon Williams applies dip and pour glaze to sturdy bone dry greenware wheel thrown P'Clay. The bone dry is almost as water absorbent as a bisque ware so a time and money saving one-fire is feasible.*

At long last, blends of pugged Potter's P'Clays® are available. It was not so long ago that features of paper clay were unknown and thus, unavailable. These blends may suit the production or hobby potter who trims at leather hard in the traditional way and who requires a body with far less pulp in it. The form of pulp used in the Potter's prepared P'Clay® is nearly impossible to recycle in the average person's studio. It differs from pulp recommended for sculpture, and is used in lesser amounts.

The Potter's standard blend P'Clay® feels more "claylike" than Sculptor's blend. Potter's has slightly less green strength, at bone dry, if compared to green strength of Sculptor's blend, at bone dry. If this direction interests you, a general reader, years of serious practice and study are required.

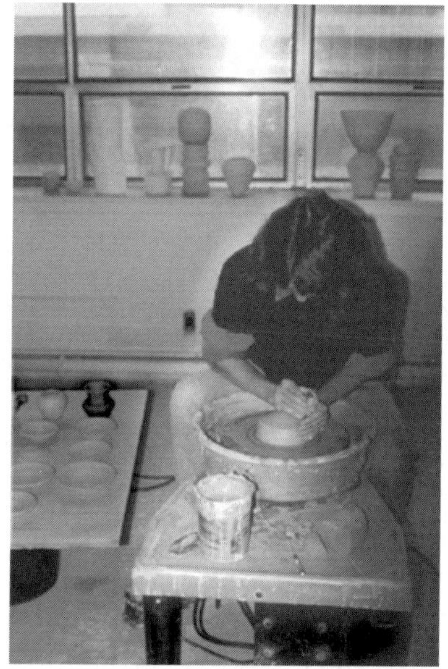

With a Potter's Wheel: *C. Resnick at wheel, in author's studio, surrounded by author's production pots small and large in stoneware Potter's Blend P'Clay® from Clay Art Center.*

Chapter five

About "Paper" in Ceramic Clays

5

About Pulp for Paper Clay

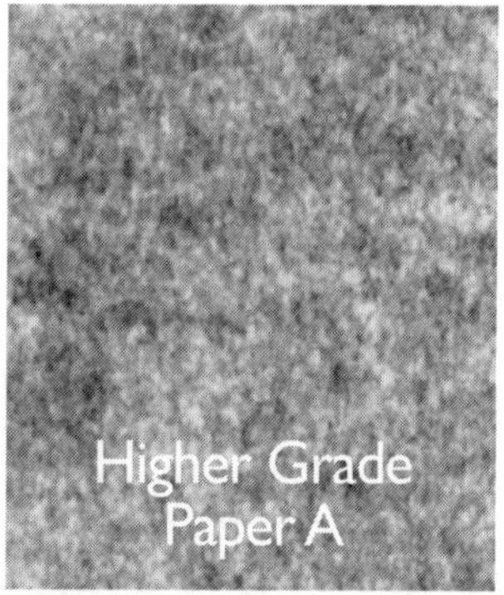

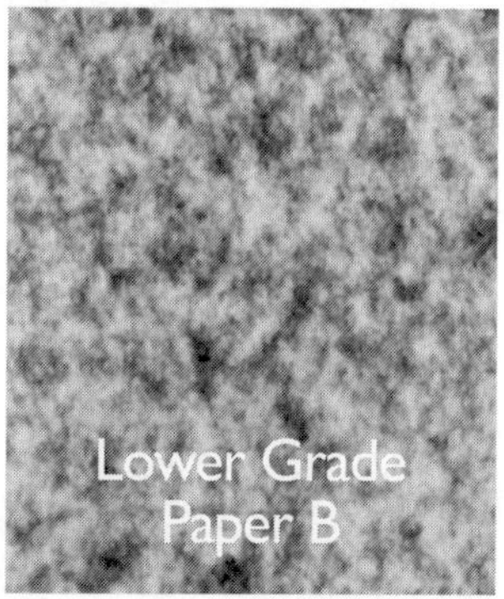

Where do I find pulp?

Paper must be broken down or dispersed into "pulp" as loose fibers in water before you add it to clay. Many household papers are suitable to recycle. To help select which paper can be good to recycle, distinctions between common papers are explained here. A paper selection chart is on page 111.

What is paper composed of?

The prime ingredient in paper is the vegetable fiber cellulose. Paper, under a microscope, looks like a web of many interwoven cellulose fibers as seen on page 79. Cellulose has been of little interest to ceramic science in the past mainly because most all of it ultimately evaporates in the fire. Nonetheless, it has a beneficial effect on clay bodies during the plastic and green states, which is worth consideration for a ceramic sculptor.

What is cellulose?

Cellulose is simply a hollow flexible tube-like structure, tapered at the ends. It's main purpose is to efficiently siphon water up from the earth to the leaves of the plant. The fiber is extremely water absorbent, spongy, and resilient to stresses such as compression, beating,

---

Fig. 76A and 76B: ***Judge Between Papers:*** *Hold two sheets of paper up to the light. One may be able to see how cellulose fiber in lower grades of paper like sample B are loosely knit compared to closer knit fiber in grades like sample A. This quick visual may help the studio artist tell which paper is faster to to recycle back to a pulp state.*

and twisting. The surface of the tube is not smooth. These characteristics make it an excellent additive to sculptors' clay and ceramic materials.

Where does cellulose come from?

Cellulose fiber, a natural by-product of photosynthesis in plants and trees, is a main ingredient in most commercial papers. Common sources of fibers used in papers are: cotton linters, linen, flax, hardwoods and softwoods. Under extreme magnification, many different sizes, varieties, and interweaving of cellulose fiber are visible in both the original plant and the man-made paper.

What is lignin?

Around each absorbent, hollow cellulose "tube" is a thin layer of water repellent adhesive substance called lignin. Each type of cellulose has a its own amount of lignin. Lignin is acidic, and causes yellowing in papers and newsprint. Thus, the amount of lignin in a paper is a concern for archival and art paper makers. Lignin found in paper clay pulp is harmless to ceramic. Lignin burns away, but it's presence or absence can affect the amount of pulp needed in the clay recipe. A chart in the appendix compares the lignin in cotton, linen, flax, and wood papers that are sources of the pulp.

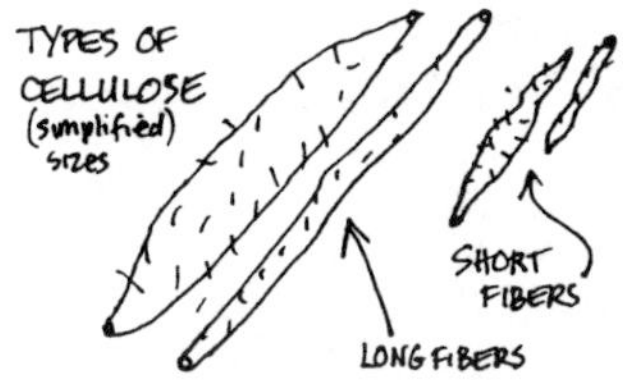

*Above: **The Tapered Tube Shape:** Any hollow individual cellulose fiber, whether from cotton, flax, linen, soft, or hard wood, tapers at its ends, no matter what length, or diameter, it is, and no matter how thick, or thin, the water absorbent cell walls of the cellulose fiber are.*

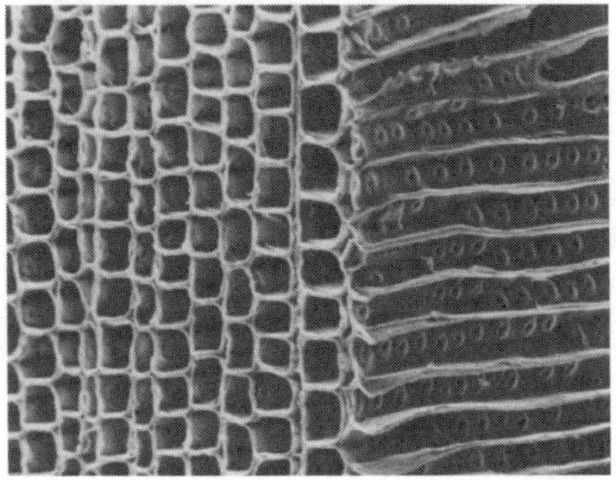

*Fig. 77B: **Internal Structure of Wood:** Every source of natural cellulose fiber is a collection of hollow tubes in some form. This SEM micrograph of pine wood (a lower grade paper source) can be a inspiration for sculptors at large scale. A practical honeycomb scaffolding of tubes may help big bone dried forms.*

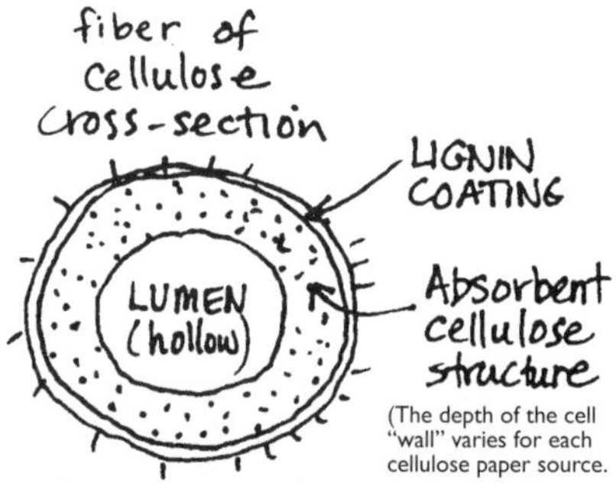

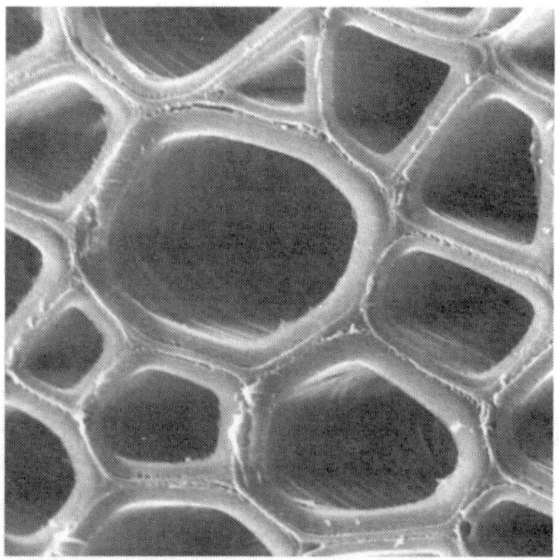

How do papers compare in cellulose and lignin content?

Of all types of paper, cotton linters contain the least amount of lignin (1%), linen flax (5%) and softwoods and hardwoods contain more, about 20% to 30%. Types of paper also vary according how much pure cellulose or hemi-cellulose is present. Cotton linters contain the most pure cellulose (96%). Flax (85%) as well as hard and softwoods (40-50%) contain noticeably less (Whitney: 1979).

Fig. 78A: ***Lignin and Lumen:*** *A white border line of "lignin" grips between the outer edges of each hollow cellulose tube to make a structure in this micrograph of aspen hardwood (SEM 1760x). If lignin, or ink, is in our paper, it will just burn out in the fire. Inferior pulp with high lignin, or too much ink can function in paperclay. See analysis in appendix.*

Does the type of cellulose fiber affect the water absorbency of a pulp?

Yes, when manufactured papers are reduced to pulp, the water absorbency of the pulp will vary according to how many lignins and what forms of cellulose are present in the original paper recipe.

How do clay particles and cellulose fibers compare in size and appearance?

When extreme close-up images of kaolin particles (from clay) are shown next to cotton linter fibers (from paper), structural differences between them are obvious. Flat slab-like particles of kaolin look much in miniature like the rocky minerals and shale they add up to in the large. Cellulose fibers, likewise, under the microscope, look tubular and branch-like, intertwining, and tangle with each other as roots do in the earth, or tree branches in the winter sky. Kaolin parti-

A Close Look at Cellulose Variations in Papers

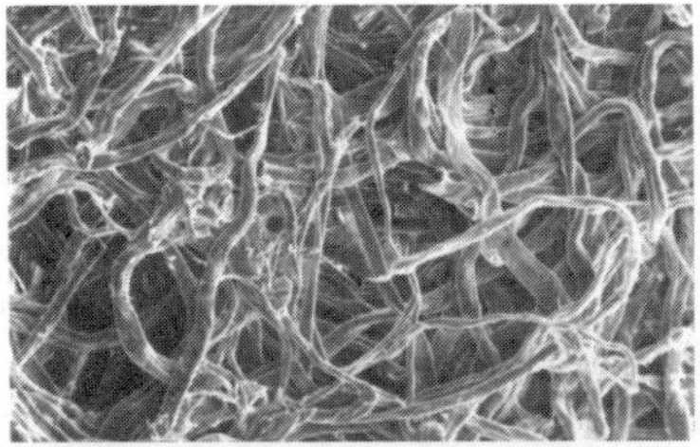

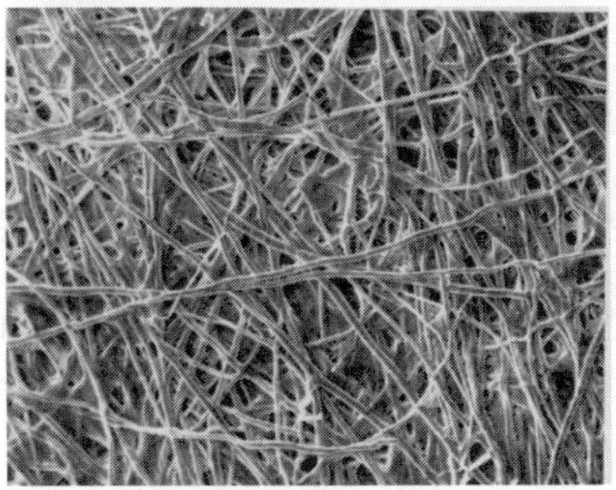

Fig 79A above: ***Raw Cotton Linter:*** close-up view of a paper like sheet of cellulose fibers. (SEM 47x)

Fig. 79B below: ***Mitsumata Paper*** has long fiber, is more difficult to untangle, and therefore very difficult to turn back into pulp. (SEM 115x)

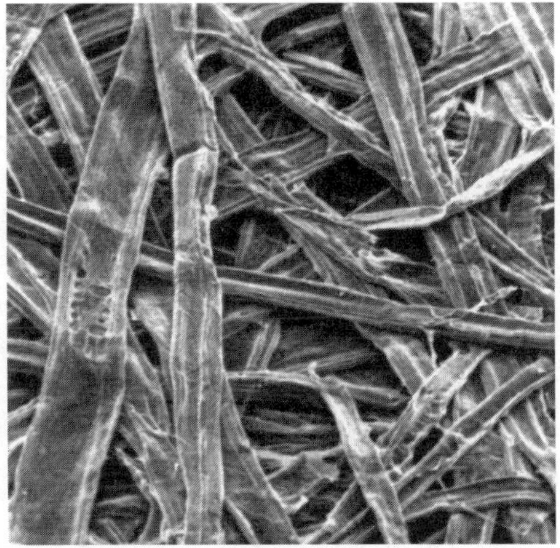

Fig. 79C: ***Flatten Cellulose Fiber:*** *Roll down wet cotton linter paper (Fig 79A) to compress and flatten tubes of cellulose fiber within it. SEM micrographs here 115x.*

Note irregular variations in size and diameter of cotton linter paper. Moreover, even at a more close up view on page 80, each fiber appears to be wrapped in a net of ultra tiny cellulose fibrils.

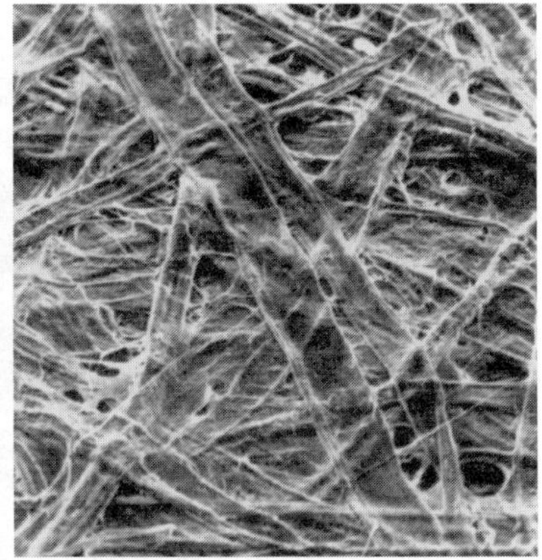

Fig. 79D: ***Ultra Flat Cellulose Fiber****: Same paper in Fig. 79A and 79C now shown after a high pressure vacuum assisted rolling. Cellulose is so resilient, it could "recover" it's tube shape from this harsh treatment if soaked in water again, though not easily.*

Note for Burnished Paperclay: *As you rub a paper clay surface, you flatten, compress, and close down openings in cellulose fibers near the surface.*

cles are miniscule. They average between 0.1 to 10 microns long. One micron equals 0.001 of a mm. In comparison, paper fibers are relatively huge. Cotton linters measure from 0.5 mm up to 6 mm in length.

Will the type of cellulose fiber in the pulp affect the recipe for paper clay?

Yes, the specific paper you select as a source for a specific pulp affects the recipe. Recipes are shown in "volume" so each maker can easily substitute one

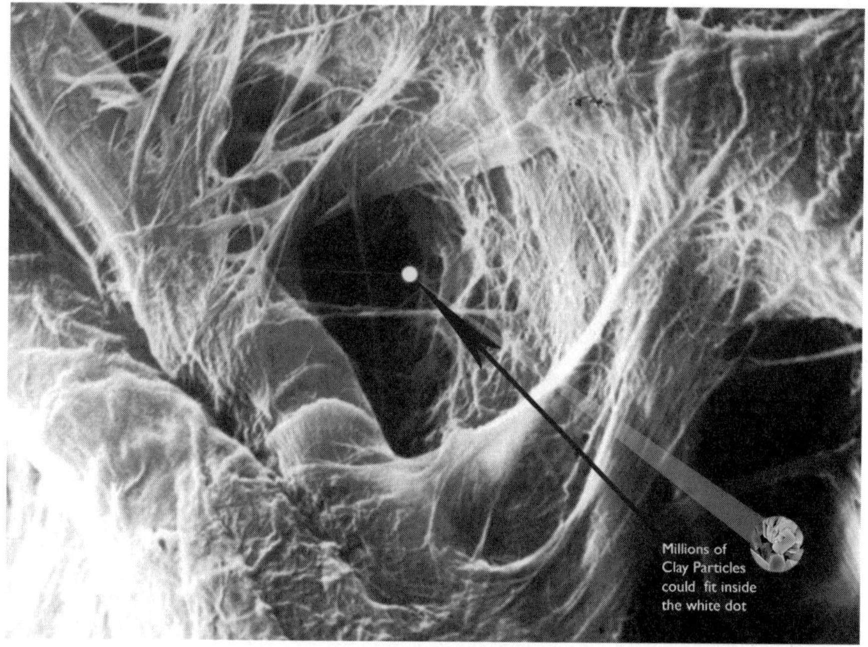

Fig. 80 to right: ***Micro-Filaments:*** *At extreme close-up, a netting of miniature branches wraps around each cellulose fiber. Likewise, the burnout voids in paperclay will be just as complex.*

A Well "Beaten" Cotton Paper Fiber Close Up: *Clay particles can fit and lodge in countless gaps between cellulose fibers, here 2250 x magnified. Up to 30% clay is added to paper recipes to smooth out fibrous textures. (Photo: Roy Whitney)*

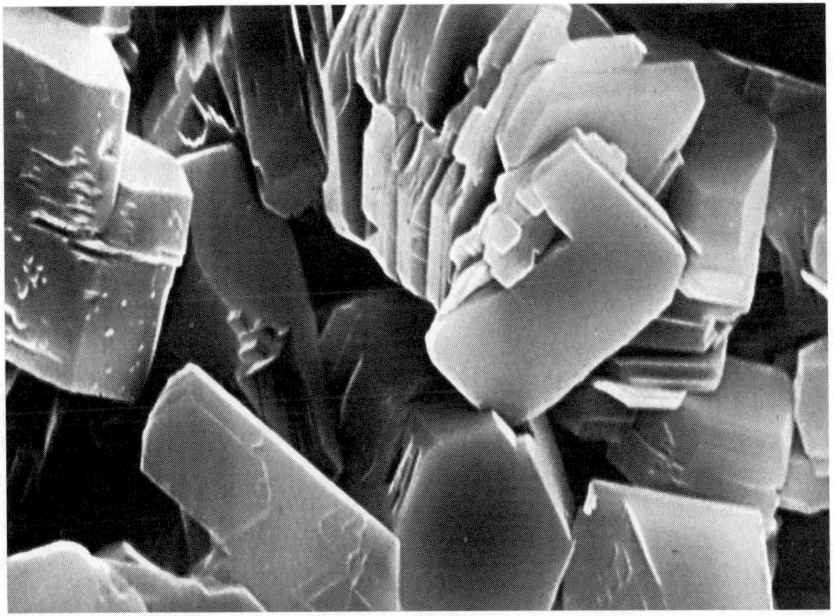

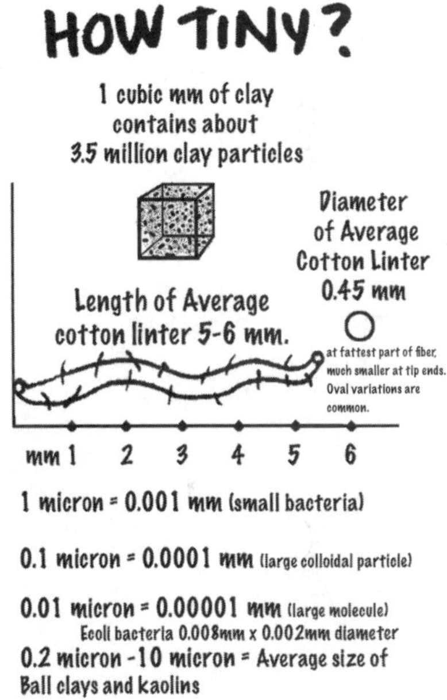

Fig. 81: ***Ultra Small Kaolin Clay Particles:*** *SEM by Walter Keller confirm the benefits of typical "aged" soft clays. Even so, dried clay chips like these are extremely vulnerable to fracture. As water evaporates there is nothing to mediate stress cracks either. In soft clay, moisture surrounding these micro-flakes helps for potters wheel work. Wet soaking (aging) and periodic wedging are needed to improve plasticity too. In the end, only the heat of a kiln fire melts particles in a clay mass together into vitreous durable ceramic.*

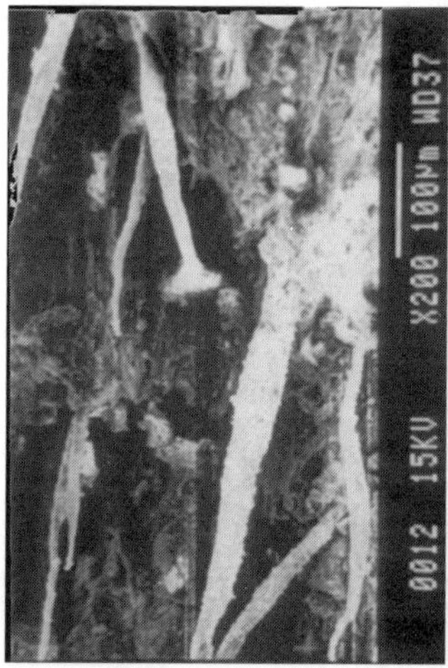

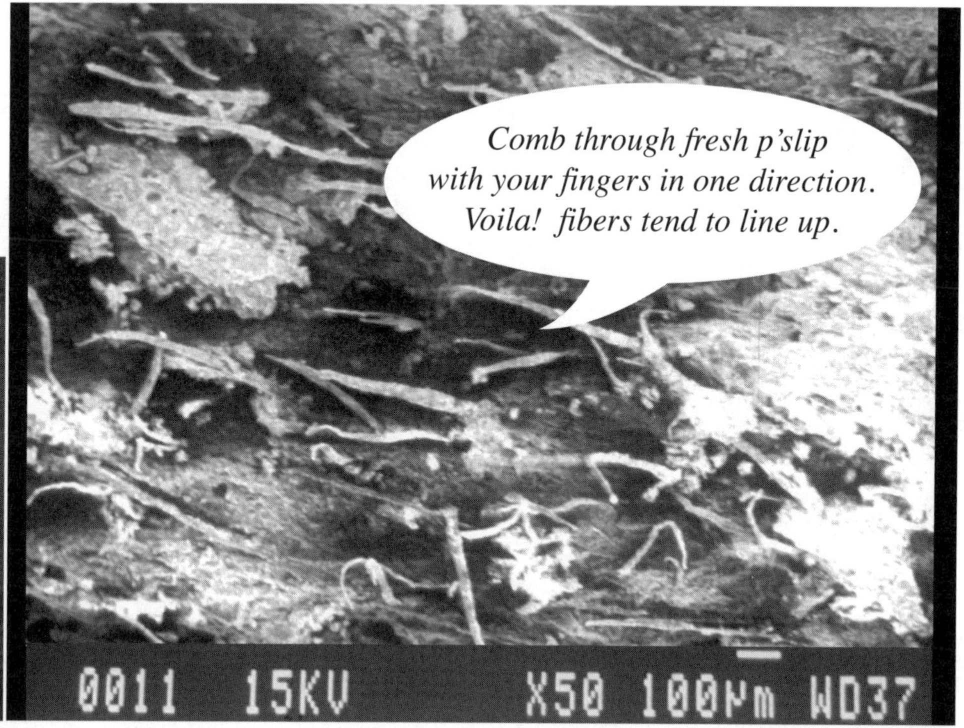

Bone Dry State Paperclay:
A chance to see the tapered ends of individual textured cellulose fibers. Masses of clay particles surround each one. Dried fibers absorb water, stretch and flex as clay shrinks and/or expands in drying cycles.

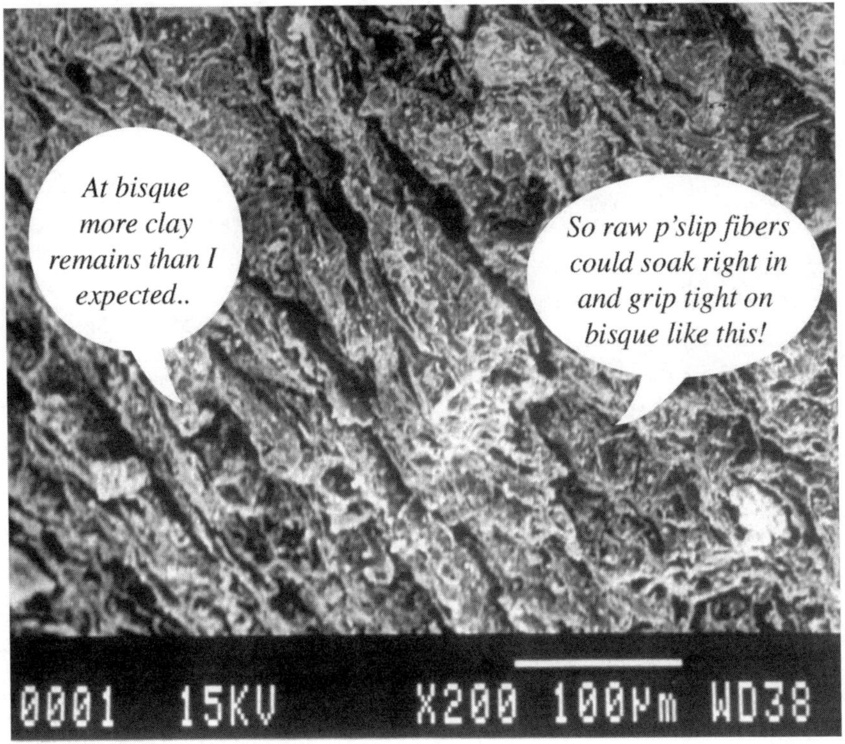

After: A Low-Fired Paperclay:

Plenty of clay mass remains at the low (700C) temperature though the fiber itself is burned away. Still, the basic internal capillary network structure of the fiber stays put. Nevertheless, just as in traditional ceramic, higher temperatures would be needed to vitrify the clay body minerals and/or to fuse glaze coatings.

Notice ***both*** *bone dried and fired paperclay surfaces remain "open" enough to accept coatings of glaze and/ or P'Slip slurries.*

It's possible before fire, to influence not just the alignment, orientation and density of the fibers, but also, to compress the round fiber to an oval fiber and therefore restrict the size of the apertures of cellulose tubes if desired for filtration and other application.

SEM micrographs Courtesy David Kingery taken from my "high volume pulp/clay ratio" mixture sample.

Cross Section: Layer of P'slip on top of bone dry Paperclay

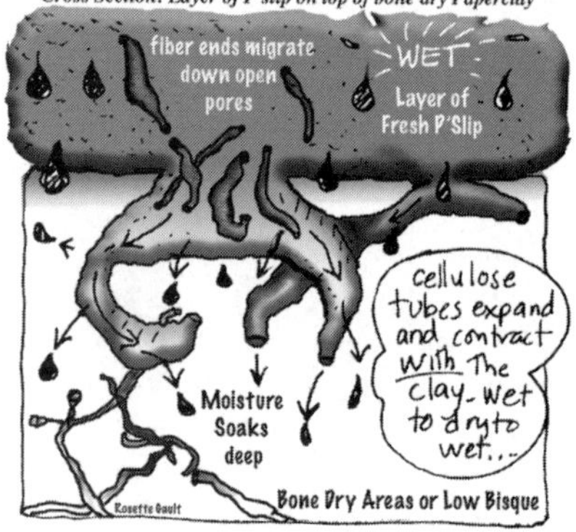

pulp for another and get the same result in terms of workability and fired result.

In general, use more volume of pulp made from papers that have lots of lignin to get the same loft and properties as a smaller amount of pulp from a high cellulose and low lignin paper. Paper clay, made from high cellulose cotton linters, has a slightly different fired internal density than the paper clay made from lower grade paper. This subject is worth more specific research.

How Paper Clay Heals

What happens to dried paper clay if a layer of wet paper clay is poured over top?

Hollow tubes of absorbent, "thirsty" cellulose that reach the surface of the dried out paper clay start to soak up the available water from the fresh paper clay slurry. These tubes perform as a network of tiny roots in the clay body to distribute the moisture in a capillary action over a wide internal surface area.

The cellulose fibers in the dried paper clay body expand and contract, each time the paper clay dries and more wet mud or slurry is added. The bond between both the older and newer layers of paper clay is surprisingly strong, provided the ratio of pulp to clay is adequate.

If stress cracks begin to form in paper clay, what difference can fiber make?

In a balanced matrix of fiber and clay, fibers tend to interrupt and eventually stop stress or shrinkage cracks in their tracks. Fibers used for this purpose improve the green and sometimes also the fired strength of clays. Nylon or fiberglass fibers commonly used in the past are relatively large, smooth, uniform and costly. These do not compare in size, or variety to the much smaller, delicate, hollow, resilient, water absorbent, compressible, as rough textured cellulose fibers found in paper pulp. When a crack starts, more energy is needed to pull a cellulose fiber out of its track than you would expect. The rough micro-surface of paper is seen page 80.

Both man made and cellulose fiber help green strength. Why would cellulose be any better?

Man-made fiber is not alive. If stored in water over time it is nearly inert. It has been used in the years when the process of aging clay gave water enough time to soak deeply between clay particles.

Man made fibers are formed by extrusion. Therefore there is no extra function in a clay other than to take up space. They do not draw or mediate a flow of water and/or air through a mass of clay particles like cellulose can. Also, the surface of most all counterfeit fiber is uniform and smooth. Clay particles can't lodge embed in the surfaces of the fiber so the burnout void result, when there is one, is also much smoother.

Man-made fibers do not compress or expand well either. They can't flex as

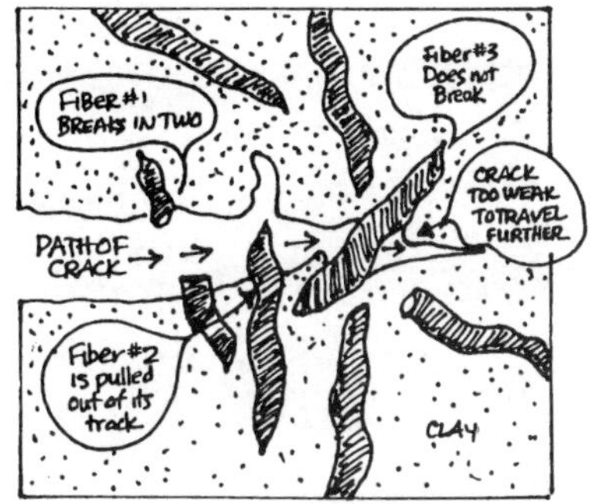

ANATOMY OF A CRACK

easily as cellulose. Cellulose fiber naturally shrinks and expands at a rate similar to clay (5-20%). Most, man made fiber does not help thermal shock capability of the fired result either. Cellulose fiber helps even the "shortest" clay withstand thermal stress of temperature extremes like freeze thaw cycles, raku, and etc.

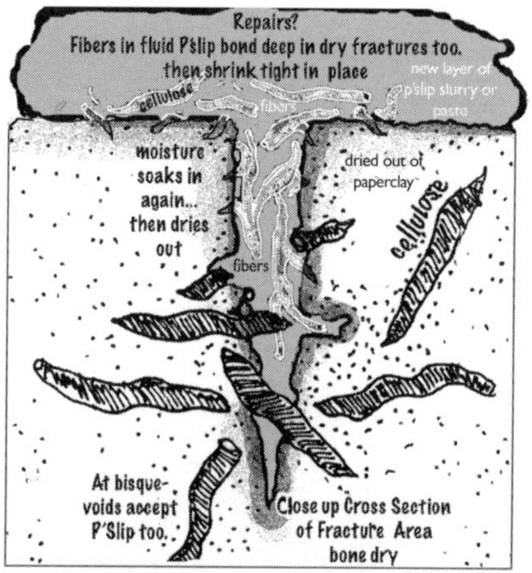

Are there more reasons to consider the use of cellulose fiber?

Plenty of inked shredded paper is free for the asking. One big bag or even a single toilet roll will make more pulp than you may need to use at first. Aside from it's attractive price and availability in the age of computers and copy centers, cellulose is tiny, hollow, water absorbent, resilient and rough along the edges. Billions of clay particles surround and grip cellulose firmly

To visualize what happens in the micro world within a bone dry paper clay contacts with P'Slip, imagine what would happen if you were to dip the end of a flexible drinking straw that is made of fuzzy terry cloth into a glass of water. The water would travel as far up the absorbent straw as it could by osmosis.

Dip a dry imaginary dry terry cloth into a bucket of clay slip. Even more clay would stick to the towel surface compared to a smooth rubber mat. Cellulose fiber at the molecular level has a tightly wound springy linear spiral structure of atoms a little like a child's "Slinky." The more I learn about the efficient design of cellulose fiber, the more I stand in absolute awe of the genius behind nature's intelligent design.

Why can't the grit in traditional granular additives (like grog, sand, sawdust, vermiculite, and etc.) Allow the wet on dry versatility of the cellulose fiber?

Sawdust bits are large compare to cellulose fibers and enormous compared to a clay particle. The wood fibers (cellulose) within each grain are a compressed tangle. They are rounded granular clumps or fragments. So is grog, ground up bits of pre-fired, pre-shrunk, inert firebrick. Before

Strength

paper clays were understood, grog, or chamotte, was successfully used to inhibit drying shrinkage, and to inhibit drying cracks. It has been used to "open" clay bodies as well. The structure of grog is essentially a granular volume. In contrast, cellulose is a linear hollow straw that permits maximum travel for moisture by osmosis due to its vastly increased absorbent interior surface area. Some people like a little of several additives in their paper clay. I personally don't care for the texture of grog because I like a smooth surface to carve on. Grog is useless in paper clay unless the artist wants the gritty texture.

How strong is paper clay as a fired ceramic?

Fired strength of a matured paper clay compares to a matured traditional clay. In most cases, if the base clay is poor, the paper can't be expected to improve its fired quality noticeably.

Strength variables include: composition of the parent clay, amount, and type of cellulose pulp in the mix, as well as the way the paper clay slip was applied and allowed to dry. Both fiber and clay particle alignment can be controlled. Another factor is whether or not the miniature tubes of cellulose in the paper clay are opened up and "round." Burnish, or surface compression, inhibits some but not all advantages of paper clay.

Generally, the fired strength will start to gradually change as the pulp to clay ratio exceeds 30% to 40% in pulp, assuming that the firing temperature is not changed. Do a test for yourself if this is a concern. With moderate amounts of pulp (volume 20% to 30%), I have not encountered noticeable differences in strength after firing, nor did Professor Kingery.

It has been my experience that the low fire paper clay recipes can usually be fired hotter than expected with success.

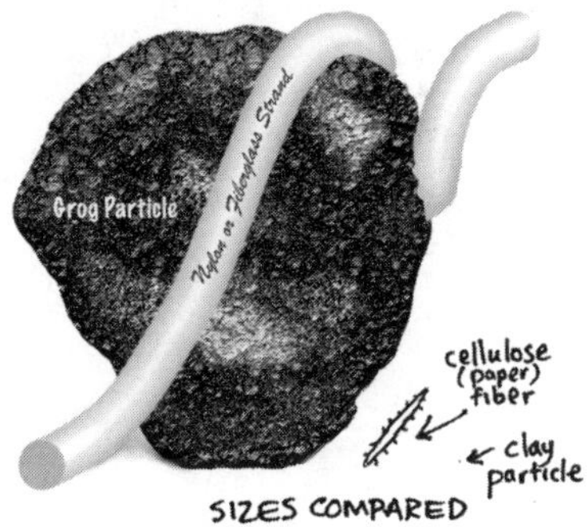

This differs from the high fire. There appears to be a cone 6 or so change in the firing effect on a paper clay body. Beyond that temperature, process of micro melting, partial glass forming, and crystal formation may occur in some types of porcelain and stoneware in certain kiln atmospheres such as salt or reduction. Certain combinations of raw materials (or eutectic) could lower the maturing point a few cones. Test fire, to know for sure what kind of high fire clay, feldspar, and pulp, you have. Minimize surprises, especially if you send thin, or delicate, structures to fire. Details are further explained in both the firing and the sculpture sections of this book.

How strong is the paper clay as green ware?

When my samples of a low fire paper clay with low and high amounts of pulp were compared to the same clay without pulp in stress tolerance tests performed by Professor David Kingery at the University of Arizona, the difference between the two was clear. To quote Professor Kingery:

> ***When the maximum load on the paper clay samples (applied pressure on the clay sample) is reached, there is not immediate fracture with a precipitous drop in the load. Instead, there's a gradual decrease in the load as the fibers are being pulled out of the enlarged crack in the fracture process. The requirement for continued applied load as the displacement extends past the initial fracture is the basic reason why these samples are mechanically superior to the purely brittle dry clay without fibers.***
>
> ***These results explain the increased toughness and greater sculptural freedom that results from the use of a clay paper composite.***

Won't the open voids leftover from each burned out fiber give paper clay a case of instant "osteoporosis"?

If the paper clay has not vitrified, yes. The micrograph of an under-fired sample of very high pulp content paper clay on page 17, shows us just how many "openings" existed at 700C. In many paper clays, micro-melting occurs along the interiors of these voids as the heat increases in kiln. More volume, less weight, and a slightly more open structure, suit raku and outdoor sculpture. Free movement and evaporation of moisture is allowed. Successful thermal expansion and contraction through episodes of not just firing stress, but extremes of season change, will be more likely.

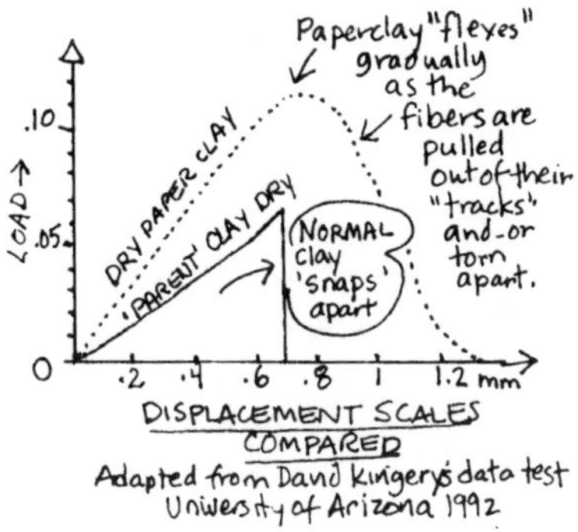

How do paper clays compare for fired water of absorption rate?

I have held in my hand fully vitrified high flux paper clay that tested nil, i.e. less than one percent water of absorbency. If you get the firing temperature right, there is no reason the water of absorption rate should differ from the parent clay. In my extensive tests, the variation between the paper clay and the non paper clay was far less than 1%.

Will paper clay stop my slabs from warping in the fire?

Beware of forming slabs and structures that are too thin for practical use when fired. Use common sense when firing thin slabs without props or support. Avoid placing thin slabs "on edge" in an "uneven" heat. A slump or warp could occur if the parent clay is at maximum maturing temperature. Use your best judgment and adjust firing temperature or slab thickness accordingly. Refer back to Chapters 2 and 3 to see detail on how flat paper clay slabs are made. For those who want one, Chapter 7 includes complete instructions for building a proper plaster slab. Don't be surprised if an old wedging plaster slab doesn't dry P'Slip out very fast, or very evenly. Sixty percent of the wedging plasters I tried in the schools and universities I lectured and taught in are too old, too saturated, very scratched up, or had been improperly prepared at the start.

Shrinkage, Fired Weight, Maturing Temperature

Does paper clay shrink like conventional clay?

Yes, in my tests, paper clay slightly retards the shrinkage of the "parent" clay. The percent change was not enough to be of significance in normal firing conditions. Chapter 3 explained how to use the shrinkage "feature" to superior advantage.

What happens when a paper clay body dries out?

The volume of both the form and cellulose fiber contract as a unit. Water absorbent cellulose tubes surrounded by the clay compress with the clay as they soak up water from *within* the clay. Evaporation, then takes place inside and outside the clay.

Do larger amounts of cellulose affect the maturing temperature of the clay?

Yes, as mentioned earlier, it depends if it's a high or low fire clay. When the ratio of pulp to clay by volume was approximately 45% most low fire base clay structures did not start to warp until around cone 4-6 temperatures, far hotter than normal. Unglazed, some over fire tests did not hold water or slump.

At heats beyond cone 6-8, some porcelains seemed to lose "structure" at the same temperature as before, but the "timing" changed. Detailed research on variables like kiln atmosphere, and melting interaction (eutectic) between minerals in the pulp and clay in question, is needed. I suspect presence of elements like magnesium, calcium, sodium, and also soluble trace minerals exacerbate this.

Shelf Life

How long does a batch of paper clay stay fresh?

Mix up what you need as you need it. After two weeks or so bacteria may grow and the mix could start to stink. To prolong its life keep the batch well covered. Certain batches of plastic wedged paper clay keep fairly well, for months and even years, if well wrapped in plastic, students report. In time the paper clay, may turn a darker color on the inside; even so, it still functions properly when used.

How long does the wet pulp, by itself, stay fresh?

Pulp can be stored in an airtight container or bag for several weeks or more. Add several tablespoons of bleach or equivalent preservative to the pulp water before straining to inhibit mold and bacteria formation. Students report that they have frozen pulp for even longer periods and thawed it out with success.

What do you do if your paper clay starts to smell?

Let it dry out. The smell will stop.

In the fifties, Robert Rauschenberg started work on a large sculpture made from a mix of paper fiber and clay in hot and humid India. After a few weeks, the clay started to smell so bad that the project had to be abandoned. Of course, as taught, he must have kept it covered with wet towels and maybe even plastic. Nowadays this problem is easy to solve. Avoid covering between work periods.

Suppose I have a bag of ready made P'Clay®, can I work with it months or years later?

Yes, I have bags of first test batch lasting over ten years so far. I do not age paper clays because they do not need it. Cellulose fibers insure good water penetration throughout the clay and

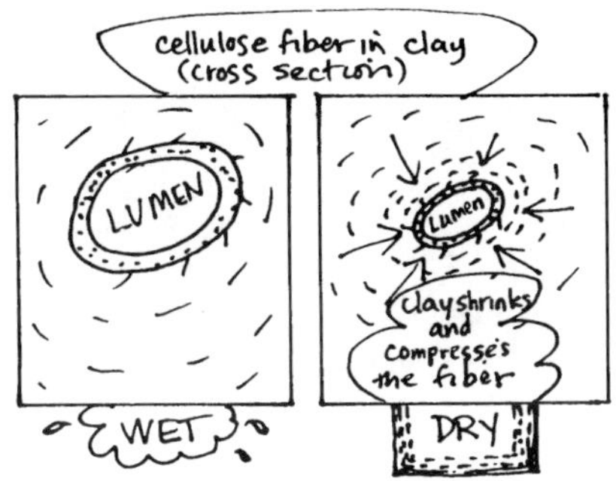

between clay particles. To avoid stiffening up in the bag over time, open the bag and squeeze a sponge load of water in the bag and then, reseal the bag. When a properly made paper clay gets "short," it's almost always due to it being too dried out, and so, too stiff to work. If this has happened, "slice" the pug up right away and dry all of it out.

Re-softening leatherhard paper clay is more trouble than its worth. It is far easier to add on fresh soft to a bone dry part and recycle small dry scraps back into P'Slip.

Why do you advise drying out all scraps of paper clay and storing these as dry slice bits instead of soaking them over time in a water slop bucket like traditional clay?

Why keep heavy buckets of "clay soaking in water" around the studio? Age no more. Thin dry bits of paper clay slake down fast (less than an hour) with less or no lumping in a bucket of water. Leather hard or wet bits are stubborn to disperse or slake. Discourage students from wadding scrap bits into leather balls for this reason. I love having a supply of thin dry scraps stored out of the way in old clay bags/boxes, light weight, easy to move, kept pure, and ready to turn into P'Slip at any time.

My dry scraps of traditional clay and paper clay look the same. How can I tell which is which? Can I recycle and slake them down in the same bucket?

To test, just dip the suspected dry part in a bucket of water, and hold it up to your ear. Listen for the soft "crinkly" sound of the water soaking deep in a bone dry paper clay. I separate paper clay scraps from traditional beforehand. Then I slake them in water separately, to avoid unintended lumps of traditional clay. Troubles, and irregular shrinkage due to uninvited lumps of traditional clay, show up at bone dry, or worse as hairline fractures, pockets, or worse in final fire.

I have some bags of fresh P'Clay left-over from a project and I know I won't have a chance to work for a while-maybe not until next summer. What's the best way of storing it until then?

I take the clay out of the bag, and shave off thin bread slices with my cutting wire. I lay the slices in the air to dry out. This stops microbe growth. I store these as long as I please in a bag, or box. When I'm ready to get back to work, the slices dissolve and slake down in a bucket of water. Within an hour, or less, I'm ready to go with P'Slip once again.

I mixed my own custom batch of P'Clay yesterday, and wedged it up as soft modeling clay. How long will it keep wrapped in plastic, or kept covered with wet cloth?

Indefinitely, kept very moist. However, I prefer to use it up within days, weeks, (or months at most,) when I want to avoid the sight or smell of microbes. A lot depends on your raw ingredients, especially the kind of pulp, temperature, humidity, and climate in your corner of the world.

I just mixed up a studio made bucket of P'Slip, but I'm not ready use all of it yet. Is there a time limit for it?

In practice, if I drape plastic directly over P'Slip down low in the bucket, it will tend to retard the tendency for changes in smell, or appearance, of the batch. Some varieties change in two weeks, and others last for months! The average is around a month or so.

When I realize it's going to be a while until I use the remains of a batch, I simply pour it all out over big plaster drying slabs, and let it go totally bone dry, like drywall sheets. Then, I store the big sheets wherever I like, until I need them. I have stored these for years. They keep indefinitely. Within an hour, I slake them back down in water for P'Slip. Flat sheets of bone dry paper clay are good for building structures, or tiles as is.

Sometimes, when the batch is not fresh made, I see, or even smell, evidence of live bacteria and/or mold on it, and sometimes it's in the modeling P'Clay®. What can I do about this?

It is clear that many pulps, especially our beloved inked "recycled" ones, and more than a few raw mined clays, contain so-called "organic" microbes that thrive in the moist humid clay bag. DNA does its work. It won't take long, weeks or months, depending on the microbe involved, before you (the giant with big eyes) can detect them. The rate is different for every single batch of P'Clay® ever made. What to do?

Choices include:

1.) *Relax,* and carry on your project. When clay dries to bone the microbes die, and the remains sizzle into oblivion during fire. Some people scrape the greenish mold off the surface of the still wet P'Clay lump with a metal rib, and go back to work. Rarely, you may see dark streaks inside the clay mass when you slice a wire through. For peace of mind test fire a little slice to be sure the dark streak(s) is not caused by some *other* non-pulp "contaminate" that would stain the fired result.

2.) Mix just enough studio batch up to use as you go. Use P'Clay fresh. It needs minimum "aging." I never add bleach or other disinfectants nowadays as they can cause skin and other irritation.

3.) If fresh P'Clay® arrived at your door in a substandard condition, get it replaced with a fresh bag, or request a discount credit to your account. All licensees agreed to deliver fresh. If you are not happy with the service, or attitude, of your manufacturer, call up as soon as your P'Clay® arrives. This helps the manufacturer know better the shelf life of that particular batch, and gives the company an opportunity to double check whether they mixed that batch right. If your issue is not resolved, you can advise me too. The substandard P'Clay® is still usable, of course, but some people have allergies to molds and microbes. If so, use fresh made mix, as I do, so there is not enough time for any of the air or water born microbes to colonize.

It has taken traditionalists more than a few years to really let go of the idea that "aging" is necessary with paper clays. Cellulose fiber delivers water near and between interior clay particles efficiently. The practical reason for "aging" of all traditional clays is clearly visible on page 81. It takes time and wedging motion to help water to seep in between dried clay particles to improve the plasticity and workability of traditional clay.

Chapter six

About Mixing Studio Paper Clay with Recycled Paper

6

Paper Recycling Sources

Where can I find good paper for use in my clay?
Most non-glossy, out-of-date printed materials are free for the asking. Papers from offices (even mixed with carbons), copy centers, computer work stations, and print shops give excellent results and fire out white. The paper this book was printed on (not including the cover) would work. For paper clay, the best papers have relatively shorter fibers, with no glosses or glues. The previous chapter explained how papers differ with extreme close up views of detail.

Certain types of drawing and blotter papers may also be used, especially if they tear apart easily. Egg cartons dissolve quite well, it's reported. These papers will dissolve to pulp in hot water within 5 to 15 minutes of stirring and agitation. Some scrap papers have already been shredded into tiny strips, which speeds the pulp making process all the more. Refer to the Paper Selection Chart on page 111 for details.

How can I tell which papers will be easier to make into pulp?
The more difficult the paper is to tear, the longer time it will take to break down to pulp. The easier the source paper is to tear, the less stirring time it will take, the "easier" the pulp making is by hand labor.

Which paper is the easiest for a beginner?
If you've never seen what wet pulp looks like, and it's your first batch, one store bought toilet roll would be good to practice with. Most brands worldwide disperse nearly instantly in cold water even, and with some you could use your bare hand to agitate

the mix into pulp. One roll goes a long way. Do not blend the cardboard tube in with the batch. It takes far too long for it to turn to pulp. Dip one entire roll into the 5 gal. or10 liter bucket of water and then peel off the layers of soaked tissue. I realize toilet paper made from recycled paper is not as popular today as the bleached ultra processed white brands. Either will work just as well in a paper clay. They fire about the same. If you stick with one brand of roll it's a good measuring method. Recycling and pulp breakdown procedure is a lot easier with other inked papers when you at least know what wet pulp should feel and look like when it's ready for the clay.

What else should I watch for in the scrap papers?

Avoid or remove envelope windows, cellophanes, waxes, plastics, glues, and staples, as these do not dissolve in water. Staples may cause a dark mark on white fired clay.

Grade and sort papers for quality, type and ease of tearing; e.g. all computer paper should be pulped up as a batch separate from pulps from the fine quality high rag drawing papers. Some types of paper dissolve more quickly than others. Each paper has its own unique characteristic.

What about printer's ink?

Most printer's inks do not affect the ceramic. Some varnishes and treatments may only affect the time it takes for the paper to dissolve into pulp. Every color of ink, Xerox, or computer print I tested disappeared in the first fire. Nevertheless, inks prepared with oxides of iron or cobalt could slightly discolor a white clay body. Test fire a small batch for peace of mind.

What happens if I try newsprint or cardboard?

These pulps are not guaranteed to fire white; some fire tan. Glues in cardboard do not dissolve quickly. This may be important to some sculptors. Many printed news prints will pulp up quite quickly, and fire white despite the dark inky grey appearance of the pulp. The plastic inks and bright colors in the advertising and magazine inserts could be slow to dissolve within an otherwise satisfactory pulp. Much depends on your mixing equipment and your particular studio setup. It used to be that most newspapers, or old phone books, pulped up easily, albeit stained dark from the ink that burned away. Nowadays, many newspapers and the like, have new colors. The new color process of laser ink are not so fast or easy to pulp up. Also longer fibers take more time than shorter ones. Pre-shredding the "colored ink" type of newsprints can help, as will a pre-soaking in the water barrel before the "beating" starts. Multicolored inks usually need multiple hot water straining through sieves in between beatings, and heavy plug-in power tools.

Why can't I use glossy papers?

You could, but these take much more time to cook and thrash into pulp than most have patience or tools for no matter how shredded they are. The gloss coatings for paper and/or ink, for example: the cover of this and many paperback books, won't dissolve in hot water easily.

To compare, non gloss coated colored or tinted papers that are matte surface typically pulp up more quickly.

Any health hazards to know when mixing pulp?

Use common sense. Although I have never personally experienced any skin rashes or allergies from pulp making and paperclay work, I often use rubber gloves to protect my skin from heat, chapping, drying, or even paper cuts, during a longer work sessions. Manufactured papers often contain additives such as bleaches, wetting agents, and even traces of clay and chalk. Mostly these chemicals will affect the PH/acid balance of the pulp water. In the studio, some of these chemicals may, in the hot water of the pulp making process, become soluble for a time. Most trace chemicals will be, in the end, either disposed with the pulp water, absorbed in the clay and/or burned away in the kiln.

Make Paper Pulp

Is it easy to make paper pulp?
Yes. With a rotary tool attached to a variable speed electric drill, stir the paper strips or paper fragments in a big barrel with plenty of hot water until they look like a thin soup of pulp. I use a hand held 3/8" power drill with a Jiffler Goldblatt Mixer Blade #130 ($25). Details on this and other tools are found on pages 110 and 111. Avoid adding disinfectants to retard growth of bacteria. When the printing is no longer legible on the fluffs of wet paper floating in the water, pour the soupy mixture over a reinforced screen to strain out excess water.
Store clumps of loosely squeezed-out wet condensed pulp in an airtight plastic bag or equivalent for later use. Pulp can be stored wet up to several weeks, and dry for several years or more.
If the paper you selected takes longer than an hour or two to break down, let the soup sit overnight, but not longer than a weekend. You may have used a paper with relatively long fibers that are more difficult to untangle. To remedy, strain and replace the cold water with a fresh batch of hot water, and resume beating. Multiple screenings and re-mixing to strain out water and break down pulp will not hurt the pulp in the least, and

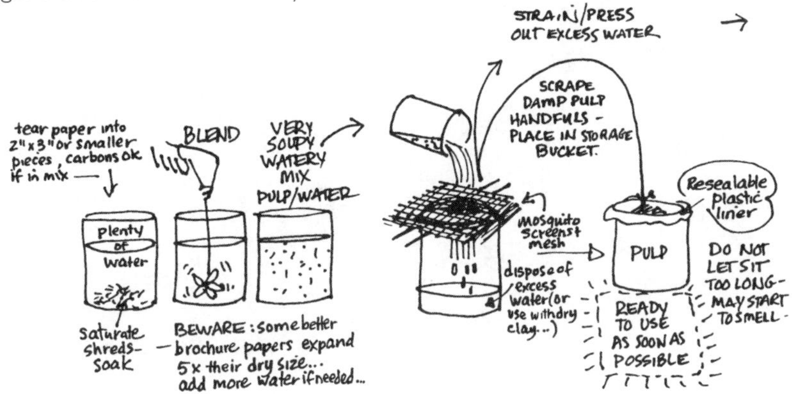

will speed the breakdown process of low grade papers and compensate for water which was not very hot to begin with.

What's a key secret to mixing up a good pulp?

A very ***generous abundance*** of hot, but NOT necessarily boiling water in a large enough mixing container. Your pulp "soup" will be thin indeed but this truly works better than thick as odd as it may seem at first.

How much water should I strain out of the pulp?

For the final screening, leave the pulp sopping wet and gloppy. This way it will disperse more quickly and easily into the clay recipe. Later, as you better understand the process, you could add dry clay directly to the pulp water, and skip the step of straining altogether. As you experiment with the consistency of pulp, you can also adjust the consistency of the slip and other variables. What's important is the end result.

What clays can you add cellulose pulp to?

Paper pulp (cellulose) can be added to any parent claybody or prepared casting slip, be it red terracotta, raku, earthenware, stoneware, porcelain, salt, or combinations of these. Glazes and firing specification of paper clay will be the same or close to those of the "parent" clay. Details about this are discussed even more chapters in my second book, ***Paper Clay*** (shown on page 121.) The exception to this advice is when you want to convert a highly modified traditional clay that is *already packed* to the maximum proportion limit with grog, sand, or other non-shrink non clay material. Granulated additives like these used to be "the only way to go" for big sculpture. The majority of so-called traditional water based sculpture clays are packed to the limit with them.

If you have one of those already on hand you have two choices: *A.)* Add more ball or kaolin clay to restore the ratio proportion of clay to non clay back within range. *B.)* Remove at least half, (or even all) of the grog from your base clay recipe so there is enough "room" to fit the pulp volume in. To avoid confusion, only the simplest success method of mixing is described here.

Is the consistency of the "parent" clay important?

Yes. Smooth slip is very important for the beginner to start with. Whether the clay source was from recycle slake down, slop bucket, or dry powder, the slurry should be thick non-lumpy creamy smooth paste. For convenience I sometimes use a pre blended casting slip stirred to honey-like and smooth consistency. Lumps of partially soft clay in the average slop bucket should be removed or else churned or strained to a smooth homogenous feel.

If you try adding pulp to lumpy traditional clay slurry, the leatherhard lumps stay as "stuck clay particle groups" that can't accept and surround each cellulose the way they

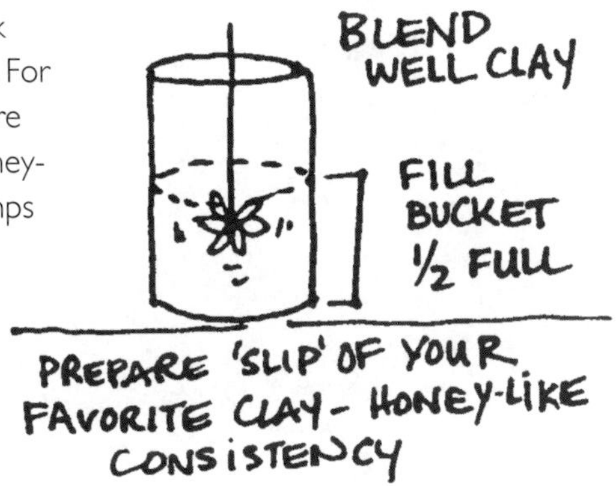

should, or rather, could! It might not be noticed at first, but later on in the work process, these mystery lumps of traditional clay in your paperclay are likely to crack, shear apart, or chip during stresses of drying and or firing. As long as you end up with a homogenous soft paper clay, you can modify the mixing system and shortcuts to suit your taste. The key idea is that the three variables: water, clay and pulp will mix together in the right balance of proportions to give makers the unlimited advantage of paper clays as shown in this book.

Could I use commercial casting slip as the base clay?
Yes, if it is more convenient for you. Casting slips work very well for me.

Why do you sometimes use casting slip, and add a dispersal agent (defloc-culent) to your clay before adding the pulp?
Adding chemicals to the water is not necessary. Nevertheless, clay particle dispersal agents/electrolytes added in slip water (sodium silicate, soda ash, darvan7 etc) serve to close up gaps between the clay particles. With ultra compact alignment of moving clay particles, and less water, the casting slip is heavier to pour and sets differently. Special end use ceramic paperclay like thin translucent sheets of porcelain, or any other ultra fine grained ceramic may require detailed attention to the interior alignment, order, and packing of clay particles between the cellulose fiber. Makers of delicate work might need to consider this fine tuning detail.

How much pulp should I add?
Calculate the approximate volume of pulp to clay by eye. Keep notes for later reference and test if necessary. For general purpose sculpture, 25% to 35% drained wet pulp to clay by VOLUME tends to gives full wet on dry feature. Benefit will still be noticed at lesser (10-25% pulp volume) proportions just expect to have more drying cracks to repair. The exact proportion varies a little due to the variations in pulp, clay, and water available any given locale. The bigger the scale the more pulp I like. To get full wet on dry the proportion needs to be high enough. Pulps vary. A 20% high rag or cellulose pulp (from high quality brochures, or purchased pure) is roughly equivalent to 28% or 30% lower cellulose pulp from shredded

computer paper. The previous chapter explained about types of cellulose. No more than 50% of pulp by volume may be added to the parent clay for wall installations and situations where light weight and a more porous and open claybody is acceptable. When the ratio of pulp to clay is between 30% to 50%, fired tensile strength of the parent clay may be reduced. Try firing the claybody a few cones higher to find a good vitrification temperature for the parent claybody, or adjust the amount of flux in the parent recipe, to compensate for openness of the body, and/or unknown amounts of clay found in the paper. Most artists won't need more control over other ceramic variables, than this. *Paper Clay* my other book, contains more detail on calculation, if you need it.

How do I measure this easily?

One method is to poke a clean ruler down into the mixing bucket full of slip, measure level, then add pulp so level rises on the ruler as much as you desire. Do not fuss over exact percentages if, for example, you are short of prepared pulp or added a lot more than intended. I use a calculator and tape "label" on the bucket to avoid confusion later. For consistent

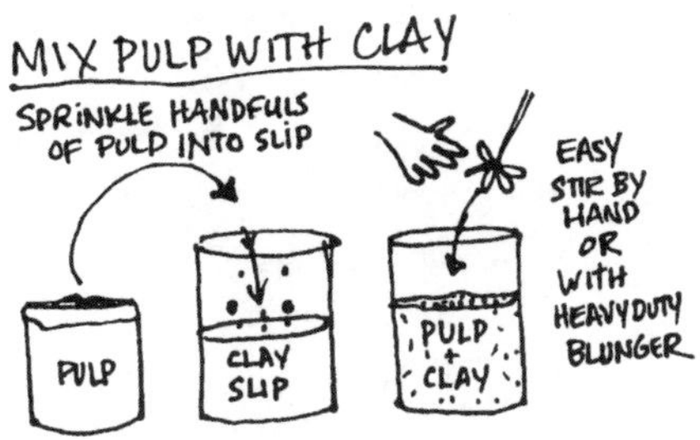

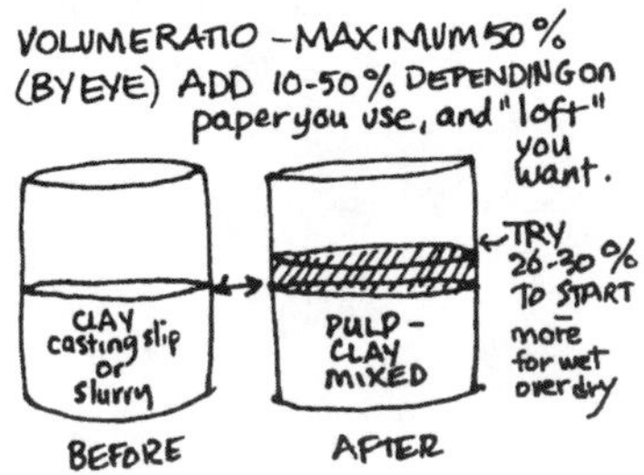

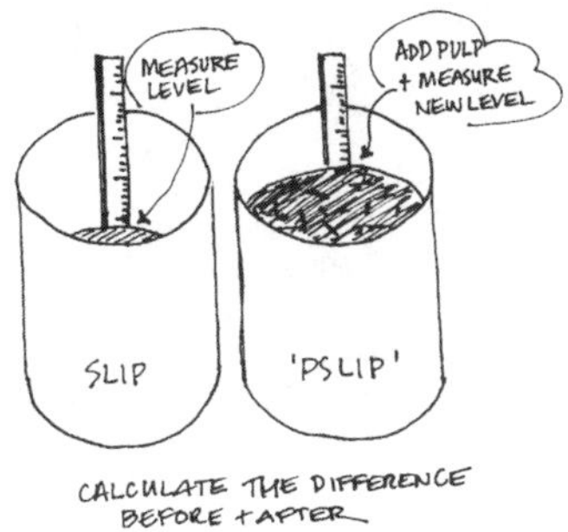

results, use pulp of a similar wetness (by eye) each time you measure for a batch.

Will I need tools to stir the pulp into the clay?

Not necessarily, hand stir until the mix looks and feels like oatmeal. Or use a power tool. I visualize a network of fibers like capillary ducts, each one surrounded by billions of clay particles like the pictures seen earlier on pages 80 and 81.

How watery can the "oatmeal" be?

The P'Slip "porridge" can be as thick as a paste of cake icing, or as thin as a soup. Obviously, the thinner the P'Slip is, the more water, hence, the more time it will take for the water to evaporate enough to model. But thinned P'Slip can be great for adhesive. My own preference is to mix a batch as a thick paste. Then, I can model with it sooner, since it takes less time to stiffen up on the plaster. If the P'Slip has lots of pulp in it, it's a fabulous smear that dries out crack free. Uses include 'making waves" such as those you saw on page 24, or for smearing a fingerpaint style surface texture as you see in the form on page123.

If I mixed up a watery batch, are there any shortcuts?

Leave the bucket a while. Sponge off as much of the residual water at the top before you stir the thicker paste that settled underneath.

How and when can I "speed" wedge?

"Speed wedge" P'Slip by the hand full for instant P'Clay soon after the pour. One way to do this is with a soft rubber rib. Scrape off strips of very soft clay as soon as you see the gloss from the water is gone from the surface and ball them to wedge. The photo (27A) on page 27 shows a first puddle pour. If you pour a thicker layer, wait a little, or a lot, longer depending on your drying slab surface. But don't let the "dry out" go too far, or the new P'Clay may stiffen too much to coil or model easily. If this happens, slice the 'too-stiff" lump upon discovery of the problem. Let, or force, slices to dry separately. It can be faster and less messy to re-wedge from slurry. Paperclay during the leather hard time can be really tough to toy with.

Chapter seven

More From My Notebooks

7

Notebook Quick Find

Firing

Can I "fire" paperclay the same as a traditional clay? Can I high fire, reduction, salt, soda, or wood fire paperclay?

Yes. Like traditional clay, beware of over fire. Some base porcelain recipes ought to be in cooler parts of a kiln, test yours to see.

Could I low fire, or mid fire, raku, pit, saw-dust, or saggar fire paperclay?

Raku or pit fire firing subjects paperclay to dramatic change of temperature or "shock." Any balanced recipe of high pulp paper clay even a non grog, non grit, non sand, minimal "casting slip" of either ball-talc earthenware or porcelain balanced with enough pulp will usually survive. Also, paperclay allows open flame firing methods that are not possible in traditional clay.

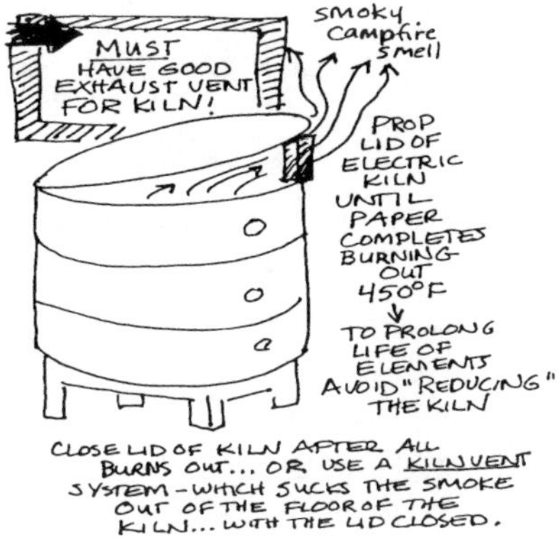

How long does it take for the paper burn out stage?

The one time 1-2 hour process begins as the temperature of the paperclay rises past the boiling point of water. To compare, the burnout of wax resists will happen during the same stage and also gives a tell-tale smell.

What are paper burnout fumes like?

If your kiln is ventilated with a functional exhaust system, or is outdoors, there may not be a smell of paper burning for an hour or two. To compare, fumes from crumpled up paper in an electric kiln are much worse.

Is a higher bisque temperature important?

If the final bisque temperature is too low, (i.e. cone 08 for a stoneware or porcelain), the bisque fired result could easily be too fragile or immature to handle. To avoid or to correct this, bisque fire hotter than normal, to at least 1000 C (i.e. to cone 04 or so).

Can I mix paperclay with non paperclay in the kiln? Could I also fire green paperclay with glazed ware in the same kiln?

Yes, fire with non paperclay is OK. Also both fired and glazed paperclay can be in the same kiln. In the same kiln for lowfire cone 04, one can load the lower shelves with glazed work and the top shelves with the dried green ware planned to fire to the same temperature.

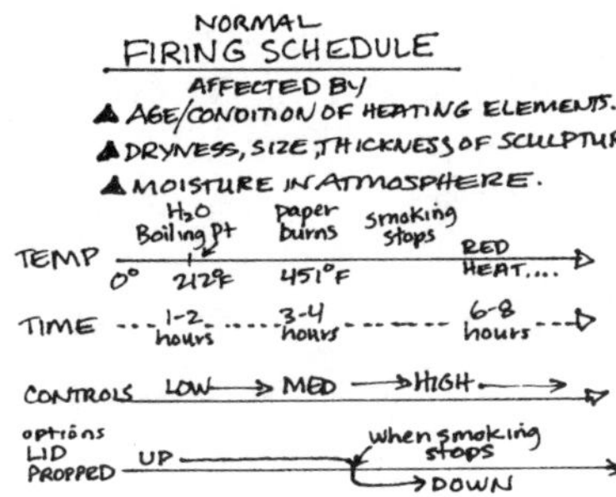

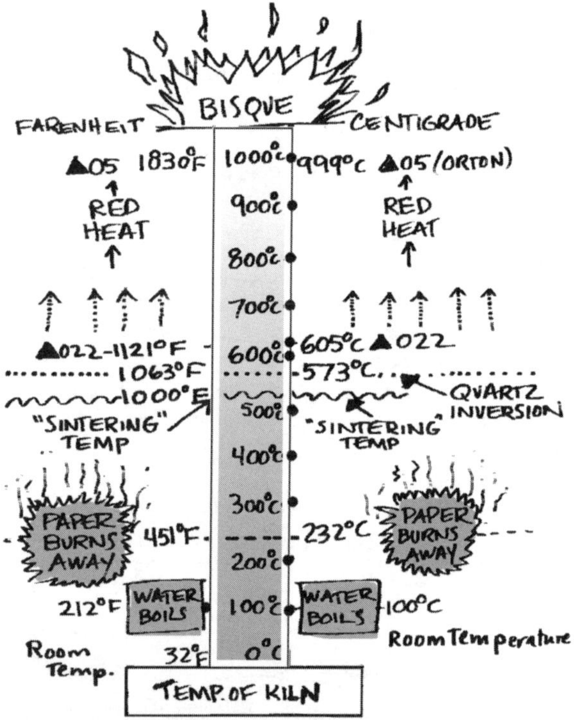

EARLY STAGES OF A FIRING

Does the presence of smoke from paper burning in the electric kiln shorten the life expectancy of the heating elements?

It depends on whether the paper has been changed to into separated pulp fiber embedded "inside the clay body" or not. Paper wads for stuffing are not the same.

For paperclay kilns, at the start of the heating period, the atmosphere inside the kiln is not even close to red hot. Steam and gases including "smoke" from pulp in clay bodies released at this stage are not hot enough to damage kiln elements. If you have a "kiln vent system," follow the suggestions by the manufacturer. If not, prop the lid and keep the peep holes open as shown in the illustration for the first few hours of fire to insure complete combustion and exit of the "paper fiber" before glazes start to melt.

By the last hour(s) of the fire, *only empty voids exist in the paperclay body where the pulp used to be,* yet air enclosed in the kiln for hours has turned into a superheated red hot gas. At red heat like this any combustible like ordinary crumpled paper ignites instantly with by product fumes that corrode the metal on the kiln heating coils over time.

What about firing of string, twines, fabrics, or twigs dipped in P'slip?

Be sure your kiln is well vented. Expect to find a hollow void where the string or twig used to be after the fire. Multiple dip twigs, leaves, etc., so the fired "shell" has a thicker wall and is less fragile to handle.

Can I fire with glass, metals, chicken wire, foam rubber, or other non-clay material?

Even trace amounts of plastic, rubber, styrofoam, polyethylene, and the like, generate toxic fumes in a fire. Avoid them.

Kiln fired metal is ***not*** *for most schools, community centers, or children*. Metal fumes can be toxic, and should be avoided by all but the most careful and experienced makers with the best possible ventilation and equipment.

Even so, both glass and metals bond firmly with most "high pulp" paper clays. Those who want to melt glass chips, marbles, and etc., might test fire at *cone 1* and fine tune the melting from there.

Burnout copper wire leaves a dark cloudy foot print in the clay. Some chicken wires and sculpture meshes are OK at low fires. Test. Saggar fire techniques with metal wraps can give flashing spray effects. Also, some metals will bisque, or raku quite well.

Any special cautions for those who mix batches with dry bagged recycled paper fiber from the local building materials supply?

Beware pre-treated "fireproofed" dried pulp building material. Why? Toxic fumes from *fire proof chemicals (like borax etc) slow down the time of burnout*. These smoke for 10-12 hours instead of the of normal 1-2!

I don't have a kiln, could I just fire pieces outdoors in an open fire or barbecue pit?

Yes, try with hand size small works and allow an afternoon for this. Bring leather work gloves, eye protection, extra long barbecue tongs, water, hand towel, and clay tools. Supervise children at all times.

1. Start fire to let hot coals and ash build up. Meantime, hand build soft pinch pots, beads, medallions, etc. nearby. Or, bring dried forms made earlier. Burnish or apply colored slips, etc. if desired. To dry, set pots near the heat, turn them every 15 minutes like marshmallows or toast.

4. When the pots are warm to the touch and dry, with leather gloves and a long stick, gently nudge these closer and closer to the fire and to the coals turning them in stages. The properly balanced paperclay is strong enough to tease gradually into the fire where a traditional clay is too fragile. After a while near the coals, bury the hot pot directly in them.

5. After about 20 minutes (or up to hours) in the hot coal bed, use metal tongs or long stick and gloves to pull the glowing hot pieces out, smoke them (like in raku), and/or bury them in sand or dirt nearby. To cool the finished works even more quickly for take-away, douse them in a bucket of water 5-15 minutes after. If you DON'T have metal tongs or a long stick, let the pots stay under the coals until the fire is out. One could extinguish fire with water or earth even while pots remain safely buried underneath the coals. When cool, retrieve the remainder fired pots from the ash..

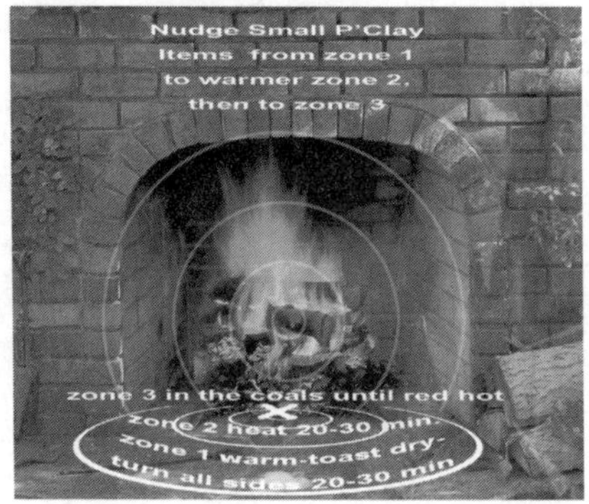

Avoid the style of mixer attachment shown below that is designed only for thin fluids like paint or thin glaze.
The blades below are too small to break fibers out of recycled paper into pulp well or quickly.

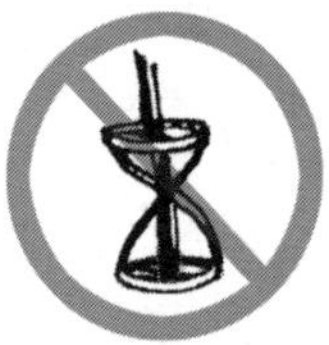

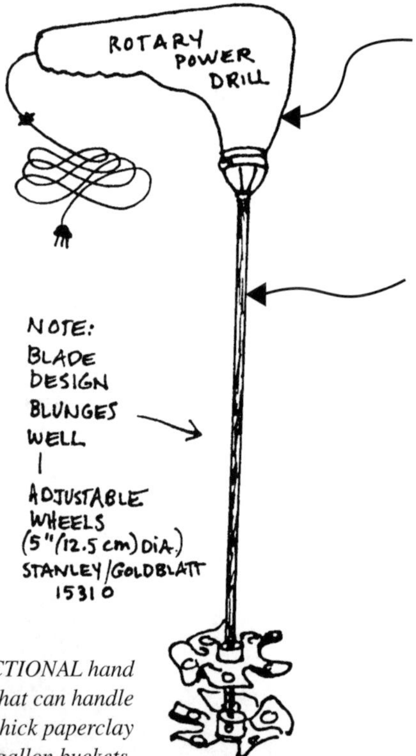

To Right: An example of a FUNCTIONAL hand held drywall mixing tool and drill that can handle both pulp breakdown and churn thick paperclay slurry (P'Slip) in 5-30 gallon buckets.

- heavy-duty **plug-in electric drill** (3/8" or 1/2" in North America, variable speed 450-1200 rpm, 4.0 amp.) Accepts shaft diameter of 100 mm to 130 mm. Most cordless drills don't have enough torque or battery power to do the job with thick slurry or pulp beating more than a few minutes. See illustration on left.

- connect a **propeller mixing blade** like this to the drill. The Stanley Goldblatt model with 5" (about 12.75 cm) adjustable wheels, 3/8" (about 80 mm to 100 mm) x 24" (61 cm) shaft Part #15310 is the best for the price and retails about $25USD. These are often available from a cement or drywall construction supply. Avoid cheaper paint/glaze mixers shown on right.

- make some large flat, smooth, clean, absorbent plaster slabs, or bats, of different sizes to pour the slurry of P'Slip on and wedge. See page 113 to read how to make some.

• screen or pulp strainer. The larger sized inexpensive kitchen strainer with a mesh of wire or plastic, and a handle, scoop well. The one I use has a no-rust plastic handle and a diameter of at least 20 cm. The strainer need not be as fine as the ones used to strain glaze materials.

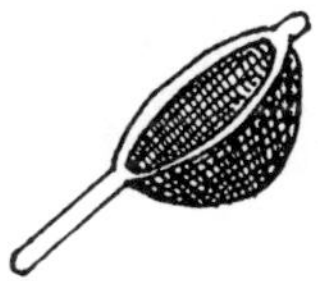

Kitchen Strainer: Used to drain extra water out of wet pulp.

• gloves, in case of scalding hot water.

• eye protection or goggles in case of spatter or splashes.

• dust masks protect your lungs from the irritation from airborne microscopic silica glass and other abrasive minerals.

Basic Hand Building Tools

To smooth and trim sculpture with

A "rib" is a simple curved flat cutout in the shape of a graceful ellipse or kidney that fits in the hand.

Three Types of Useful Rib.

a. *Rubber Rib*: A flexing soft oval like style to smooth, compress or burnish soft paperclay surfaces. Essential to aid in scraping or lifting an edge of a sheet of fresh soft paperclay off plaster surface without scratching the plaster.

b *Stainless Flex Serrated* Style: A zig-zag serrated edge all the way around won't rust, and quickly roughs surfaces for joins, texture, dotted lines, etc.

c. *Stainless Flexible Smooth Style:* won't rust, the crisp blade like edge won't nick easily. To trim with.

Tools to cut with:

1. Clean up fettle blade tool as seen on page 25.

2. Needle tool as seen on page 26.

3. Angle pointed stick as seen on page 29.

4. Slice cutting wire.

Other Tools

Small and large wipe sponges, hand towel, wooden sticks (to reach corners when fingers are too clumsy), small containers for P'Slip, a fan brush (to apply P'Slip, seen page 31), water bucket to rinse hands (size seen on page 27).

Recycled Paper

Sort papers you want to turn to pulp. The chart on the right can give you suggestions. Each type of paper has its own rate of speed when separating the fibers out of the paper into pulp so "beat" each type separately. Use plenty of water and right tools. The temperature of the water affects the rate also. Beat pulp water soup until no flecks of paper are visible.

After each type of paper is prepared separately, the resulting pulps can be measured and mixed as one pulp by volume measure when adding to smooth clay slurries.

The cellulose analysis chart below shows distinctions between cellulose, hemi-cellulose, and lignin in common paper types. Wood fiber papers full of lignin, like a newsprint, have nearly half the water absorbency of a cotton rag, linen or flax source of paper. Pulps from newsprint or "kraft" papers will not absorb as much water as pulps from cotton, linen or flax. This is why the recipe balance I recommend should be first measured in volume until a consistent suitable paper source in your studio is known to you.

Cellulose Fibers Compared (Chart via Whitney/Gault 1992)

Approximate Composition	cotton linter	linen-flax	"soft" woods	"hard" woods
Cellulose $C_6H_6O_5$	96%	85%	50%	50%
Hemi-Cellulose $C_{12}H_{23}O_{11}$	3%	10%	20%	30%
Lignins:	1%	5%	30%	20%
Recycled pulp timing varies. Some papers may need multiple episodes of agitation and beating in hot water, multiple strainings to separate cellulose fibers into a basic pulp.	Type of pulp most absorbent of water and fluffy.	Only a little less absorbent of water.	Thinner cell walls collapse more quickly when beaten into pulp	Thicker cell walls of wood pulps are sturdier so they take longer to beat or break apart into pulp. Least absorbent of water

Recycled Papers for Studio Pulp	***Sources***
Cotton linters sheets from art supply Drawing papers, trimmings if sorted Cold press easier than hot press Hot water best.	Art Studio Letterpress
Writing papers 100% rag, linen or writing bond 20-50% rag types yield less pulp for the weight. Hot water best.	Offices Schools
Uncoated NON GLOSS Book stock Out of Print Brochures on thick card stocks: great Trimmings from above Hot water best	Publishers Book Pages
Cheap copy paper, in and most colors OK, long fiber laser papers take more time. Lower grade laser tractor feed multiple part with carbons shredded, but you need more of it compared than other papers). Hot water best	Computers Copy Centers
Newsprint black and white ink preferred, old phone books. Warm water helps. Egg cartons-easy Toilet tissue rolls-easy and fastest Room or cold water OK	Household

In Studio Recycle Trouble Makers

Avoid face tissue or paper towels. Omit vellums, coated gloss, window envelopes, junk mail inserts. Beware, one stray staple, or paperclip, could ruin a smooth porcelain or worse. Rubber bands, adhesive tape and the like, are unwelcome, though harmless. Cardboard boxes: beware the glues used to laminate them take time and better tools than most of us have. Avoid pulp building material treated with fire retardant that makes noxious gas smoke in kiln.

Recycle Scrap Glaze or Clay

Scrap Glaze Reclaim:

Convert cast off ugly glaze to new life as a hard tile, brick, or dark thick surface coating.
1. Sieve off enough top water so a portion of scrap glaze (ingredient A) stirs up thick. 2. Incorporate plenty of wet sieved pulp (ingredient B) and 3. Add a portion either scrap clay, ball or china clay (ingredient C). 4.
By volume measure, test fire a mix of equal parts A- reclaim glaze, B- pulp and C- reclaim clay
Bisque fire on a protected shelf and inspect the melt. Adjust recipe to taste.

Memo: Conversion of "Sculpture" Clays

If the so called traditional "sculpture" base clay you start with feels very coarse and gritty in your hand, **rebalance the recipe when making a paperclay version**. Many traditional sculpture high grit clays are already formulated at maximum ratio between "non-clay to clay" ingredients.
At the same time you add enough pulp to make the "sculpture "clay capable of the wet over dry, also add a matching measure (or even *more* than a matching measure) of "plastic clay" (ball, kaolin, etc.) in the mix.

Recycle & Paperclay Storage

Thin dried out scraps of paperclay will absorb water, soften, and slake down if submerged in a water bucket more quickly than thick paperclay scraps. Let a slurry collect at the bottom of the bucket overnight, then pour off the water at the top. Empty the slurry on a plaster surface and wait until enough water evaporates to wedge up and model with.

For dry storage between work periods, I collect dried paperclay "rubble" and "scrappettes" in bags or old clay boxes. I use the fragments as support props, as armature parts, as stuffing, and/or as reinforcement to thicken weak weight bearing joins in already dried shapes from behind.

There is no need to age paperclay in a wet state. In the dried state it keeps.

Paperclay at the leatherhard states quickly sets up too stiff to cut or carve easily. Remainder paperclay in balls or thick pugged chunk also. Before they get too stiff to cut, slice thick lumps apart to make thin "storage tiles" like bread

Paperclay "scrappettes" can be recycled and assembled at bone dried state like a 3D collage. Periodically, to stabilize the evolving structure, an interval of time will be needed to completely force dry or air harden the new joins to bone dry. Contour with fresh soft paperclay to transform the scraps into figures as you use a sequence of workperiods to creative advantage. (Author's example to right.)

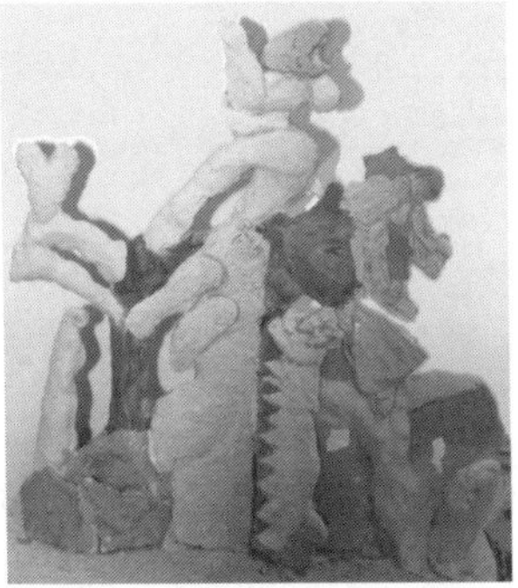

Specialty Mix P'Clays for Ultra Large Projects

If you are not sure where to start, adapt my personal recipes for life scale freestanding and wall works.

Test fire, I cannot be responsible for non-standard materials, events and results clearly beyond my control. I have indicated volumes of pulp by standard larger toilet roll to help the student with a starting measure.

1. "Rosetta Stone"

Earthenware Paper Clay for Sculpture

Cone 04 to 4 normal (maximum cone 6)

Two (2) medium buckets (use same size buckets to measure this) prepared "earthenware" base (rated cone 04-05). It can be simply buckets of prepared casting slip.

One (1) medium bucket-same size of wet strained bulk of pulp- plus or minus handfuls and inches. Dispersed paper from 8-12 rolls of "bargain" toilet tissue is equivalent to maybe 8 bulkier rolls of deluxe brands, but don't try to make this pulp in this same bucket. Use giant barrels, not for beginners to try. Master chapters 5 and 6 to avoid lumps and clumps.

What this paperclay is like to work with:
The above was my "high-fire low-fire" high pulp, all purpose, any kiln, any time, sculpture recipe for many years.

Texture before fire: Smooth, putty like. Takes underglaze, slip, engobe, stains, etc. Find surface treatment details explained in my second book *Paper Clay*.

Texture bone dry: Absorbs water when dipped. Takes underglaze, slip, engobe, stains, glaze, etc.
Thin walls soften a bit when soaked a while. Slakes down overnight or sooner.

Sinter Fired: Carves off in fine powder.

Texture after fire: Smooth, white, the higher you fire it, the more dense and hard it gets until after cone 4.

Low fire texture- Cone 03 to 04: Too hard to carve on by hand, but power tool is OK. Can treat surface with any and all commercial glazes, opaque or transparent underglazes, overglazes, etc, and refire if desired. Normal slips, engobes, stains OK. At this temperature, the result is a soft normal earthenware. Vessel will seep water without a finish gloss glaze or other seal.

Mid Range (Cone 4 to 6): Hard as a rock. Resembles white stoneware. Resists water but may not be 100% watertight. OK outdoors frost and thaw too, glazed and not glazed.

Substitutions/Adaptation:

Raku: Good anytime- bisque to 04 or more, first. When I know my kiln, the fuel, the tools, the tongs, how the shapes heat up, and where best to place them, bone dry single fire works.

China Paint, Gold, Silver and Metallic Lustre, Decal Fires: most want a cone 032. Best to apply on top of already fired gloss glazes in multiple fires.

Base Clay Options: if you substitute a iron bearing red terra cotta blended clay as base for the earthenware base, it fires red to brown. Stick to the recommended lower temperatures cone 05-02. Heavy red iron in claybody is a melting as well as coloring agent. Test samples to distinguish red clay limits compared to white clay.

2. "Porcelain Pearl"

Paper Clay for Sculpture Cone 8 plus

Two (2) medium buckets of prepared "porcelain" (cone 10) high fire casting slip.

1 medium bucket of pulp, plus or minus handfuls. (Disperse paper from 8-12 rolls of "bargain" toilet tissue equivalent to, maybe, 8 bulkier rolls of a "deluxe" brand.)

What this sculpture paperclay like to work with:

Thin areas go translucent at cone 8. Dare to fire to cone 10 only if slab walls are structurally reinforced from inside and the form is set level on the kiln shelf. For mixing batches in the studio, to avoid or minimize airborne dust clouds, start off with buckets of prepared liquid casting or pouring slip rather than large bags of dry blend powdered clay.

Texture before fire: Smooth, putty like. Takes underglaze, slip, engobe, stains, etc. per those explained in my second book Paper Clay.

Texture bone dry: Absorbs water when dipped. Thin walls soften a bit when soaked a while. Slakes down overnight or sooner. Takes underglaze, slip, engobe, stains, glaze, etc.

Texture after fire: Super smooth.

Sinter fire: Carves like soft soapstone, dense, but still easy to handle.

Biscuit fire: At cone 08 may be quite soft, handle with extreme care. Carves more like a dry cosmetic grade sponge. At higher bisque cone 03 OK to carve. Does not slake down in water.

High Fire (cone 8 to 10): Hard as a rock. If thin: walls go cone 8 and play it safe. Serious heavy duty power tools needed to alter surface.

Substitutions/Adaptation:

Base Clay Options: If you substitute stoneware throwing clay as base for the porcelain- P'Clay fires tan to brown. Reduction or oxidation atmospheres.

Raku: Good anytime. Bisque to cone 03 or more first. When I know my kiln, the fuel, the tools, the tongs, how the shapes heat up, and just where best to place them, bone dry single fire is realistic.

China Paint, Gold, Silver and Metallic Lustre, Decal Fires: Most fire to cone 032. Best to apply on top of already fired gloss glazes.

3. "Ruff-Rock"

Porcelain Ultra Short Sculpture

Cone 8-10 High Fired Texture Body

Two (2) medium buckets (5 gal./10 liter) prepared "porcelain" (cone 10) high fire casting slip

1/2 medium bucket of pulp, plus or minus handfuls. (Disperse paper from 8-12 rolls of "bargain" toilet tissue equivalent to, maybe, 8 bulkier rolls of a "deluxe" brand.)

1/2 medium bucket granular perlite, plus or minus handfuls or scoops to taste.

What RuffRock paperclay like to work with:

This is a variation of Porcelain Pearl with perlite added. It is really granular and like a mash rather than a clay in hand. It shrinks less than Pearl also.

Texture before fire: Chunky peanut butter-very short when moist. Takes underglaze, slip, engobe, stains, glaze, etc. per those explained in my second book *Paper Clay.*

Texture bone dry: Absorbs water when dipped or sprayed. Softens, then slakes when soaked over time. Takes underglaze, slip, engobe, stains, glaze, etc.

Texture after fire: Surface has openings like a coarse utility sponge, irregular granulated pocks, light weight, strong, if fired just to the right melt.

Sinter fire: Carves like frozen chunky peanut butter.

Biscuit fire: : At cone 08 may be soft, handle with extreme care. Carves more like a dry kitchen sponge. At cone 03 OK to carve but not as nice as sinter. Takes underglaze, slip, engobe, stains, glaze, etc.

High Fire (cone 8 to 10): Hard as a rock. Serious power tools needed. Gloss glaze and clay resist moisture.

Substitutions/Adaptation:

Base Clay Options: If you substitute stoneware throwing clay as base for the porcelain- fires tan to brown.

Raku: Good anytime, Bisque to cone 03 or more first. When I know my kiln, the fuel, the tools, the tongs, how the shapes heat up, and where best to place them, a bone dry single fire is fine.

China Paint, Gold, Silver and Metallic Lustre, Decal Fires: Most fire to cone 032. Best to apply on top of already fired gloss glazes.

Make a Big Plaster Work Surface

For a flat work slab up to 20"x 28" x 1" (50 cm x 70 cm x 5 cm) make a temporary frame or "cottle" form that can contain a pool of wet plaster long enough for it to set. This design can be reused for different sizes and depths of slab as many times as you want. Measure plaster the same each time for a consistent result.

A. Plan and Build the "Cottle" Ahead

Make four equal "sides:" Select or cut 4 equal sized Formica covered shelves. Measure each approx. 4" (10 cm) longer and deeper than you need. (22"-24" x 4" x 1 1/2" or 55 cm x 10 cm x 3 cm) Then, for a clamp to get a secure grip on the board, neatly attach a 1" x 1" (3 cm x 3 cm) extra end side of each board with the edge flush against the edge as shown in the diagram below with nails or screws as sketched in the diagram below.

B. Prepare a Level Surface

Locate or make a Formica covered smooth tabletop, window glass, or equivalent smooth surface. Arrange the set of frame "sides" set on edge as sketched (below right). Shim up wobbly table legs to level the cottle bottom surface. If the cottle is not perfectly level, the new pour will set up unevenly.

C. Gather Cottle Tools and Supplies:

Have ready. Four (4) clamps or clips that can clamp at least 2" (5 cm) firmly, mold release soap (not petroleum jelly) or silica spray (WD 40 or equivalent), metal rib, hammer, level, utility sponges, water bucket, moist pliant scrap clay for a putty to seal the corners and sides so walls don't leak during the plaster pour.

D. To Set up Cottle :

Follow steps 1, 2, 3, 4, 5 in order as shown on diagram. Putty in corners and edges to stop leaks when you pour. Wipe a thin coat of mold soap anywhere that wet plaster will touch. Be sure to let the bubbles on the mold soap dry completely. Mold soap should be dry but the clay "putty" be soft or leatherhard. Clean all dust out before you start.

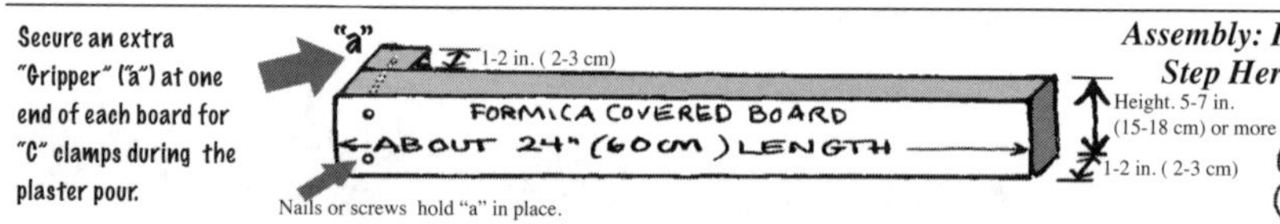

Adjustable Cottle System: Cut a set of four (4) equal planks as above to clamp together as a temporary frame. After the plaster pour sets up inside the frame, release the clamps to free the boards from the edges. Clean up wipe off any stray plaster off the edge of the Formica smooth surface right away. Use and re-use. To vary the dimensions of the frame for each slab, clamp the boards closer in, or farther apart, as seen in sketch to right.

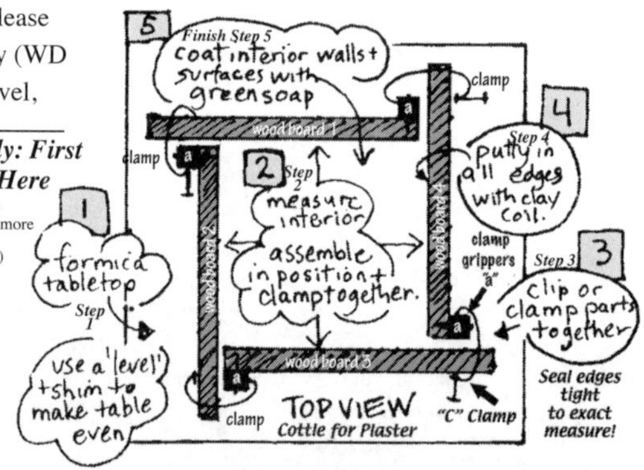

The Yield of 22 lbs (10kg) of plaster batch nearly fills a 5 gallon (20 liter) bucket and makes one large flat plaster slab (20" x 28" x 1" (50 cm x 70 cm x 3 cm) thick. If you wanted a thicker slab 2"- 3"(6-8cm) instead, then clamp the cottle walls closer together. The bucket of plaster will fill the smaller frame cottle inches higher before it sets up.

E. Is "Cottle" clean and ready? Gather Plaster, Tools and Supplies:

Have a minimum of 22 lbs (10 kg) bag of dry fresh pottery plaster, not lumpy or old. Keep the bigger bag stored in double plastic bags. Identify and mark, two 5 gallon (20 liter) buckets. Bucket One is for the water and plaster. Bucket Two is only for the dry plaster. Best to reserve these only for plaster mixing projects and never use for clay. Plaster chips contaminate clay. Don't chance it. Get all cottles (see p. 114) ready ahead, buckets clean and ready, plaster and tools together, because *once plaster meets water, you have to race the clock*. Reduce errors due to hurry or neglect with calm advance planning.

Step One Spray coat the interior of Bucket One with silicon spray (WD 40) and *let it dry*.

Step Two *Measure Water*: Fill Bucket One with 2 gallons (8 liters) of water.

Step Three *Measure Plaster*: Fill Bucket Two with 22 lbs (10kg) of DRY plaster, fluff dry plaster by stirring smooth powder by hand in bucket to "aerate" and separate dry plaster particles that might have settled (wear breathing mask).

Step Four *Mix*: Sprinkle all plaster from Bucket Two steadily over water in Bucket One as below until a small "island" appears and then soaks wet. Then, agitate by hand or with a blender 2-4 minutes (yes!) until very smooth. Now, be ready to pour. After some practice, you will know by feel the right moment to pour, ideally, just before, but not as, the mix starts to stiffen.

Step 2 and 3: Measure Water (1) and Plaster (2) Separately

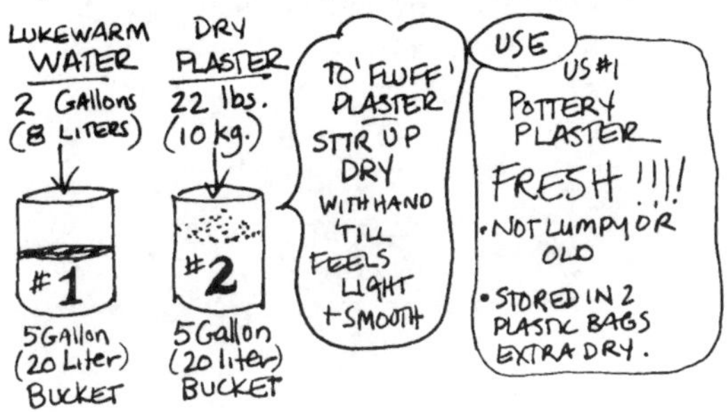

Step 4 Slowly Add Plaster from (2) to Water in Bucket 1.

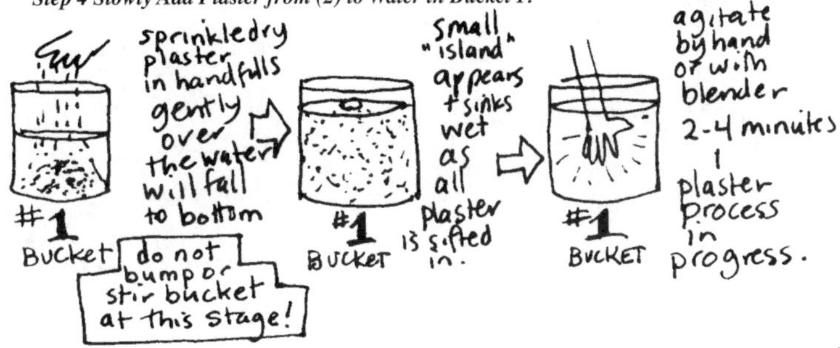

Step Five *Pour:* Let plaster pour steadily down one side of cottle but move bucket gently along the side as you pour. If you pour only in one "spot", the plaster sets up at an irregular density and water absorbency, that could show up as later as "soft spot" in every leather sheet of P'Clay peeled up off that slab. When cottle is full of liquid plaster, tap base with hammer as shown below to release air bubbles from surfaces before the set happens.

Step Six*-Cleanup:* Rinse out bucket #1 right away with plenty of running water and sponge, wipe down your tools, while the new poured plaster slab sets. Avoid pouring waste down sink drains. Rather, dispose of plaster waste water outside in open air trash.

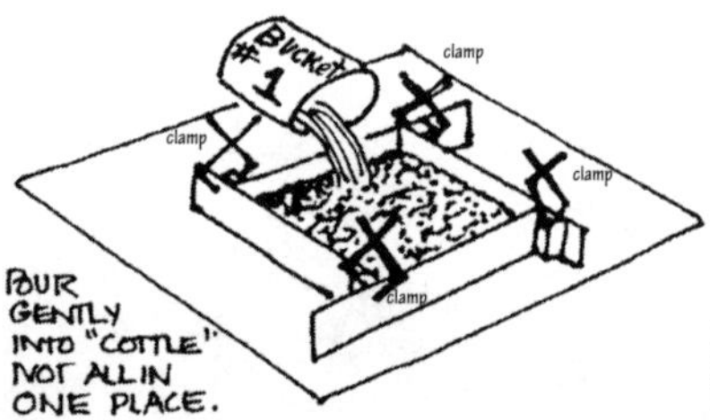

Step Seven *Gentle Release and Trim:* When plaster is warm to the touch and hardened:

1. Remove the clamps on cottle boards.

2. Gently, pry each side board of cottle away.

3. With metal rib, scrape and trim edges of new slab smooth and sponge off debris, clean with a large sponge.

4. Gently slide the new slab sideways an inch. It should release without stress. It is still fragile.

5. Lean plaster on it's side and scrape off more rough edges with a metal rib, Do not scratch fresh surface on front. Wipe clean with a damp sponge.

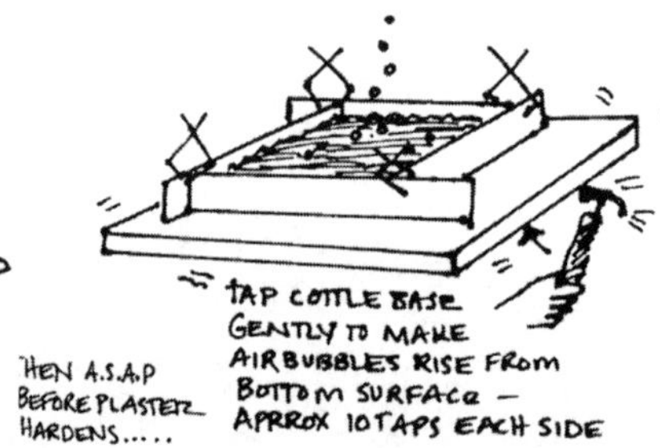

Step Eight *Days to Cure:* Let new slab dry on its side (see below) somewhere undisturbed for **about one week** in a warm, but not "hot" place. A rotating fan moving air over the surface of the slab will speed up the drying process.

Wait at least one week or more before use. Beware, the temptation of toasting the slab dry in kiln is not effective. Wet uncured plaster cannot absorb ANY water out of clay slips. When you use your slab, its nice to prop it up from below, so there is air underneath that retards mold over time as per the illustration below. Avoid use of any metal tools that scratch the surface, rubber ribs are preferred.

Important: Keep all plaster waste separate from any and all clays in studio. Once the plaster is totally cured, there should be no plaster chips likely to get loose and into your clay. These can be troublemakers after fire.

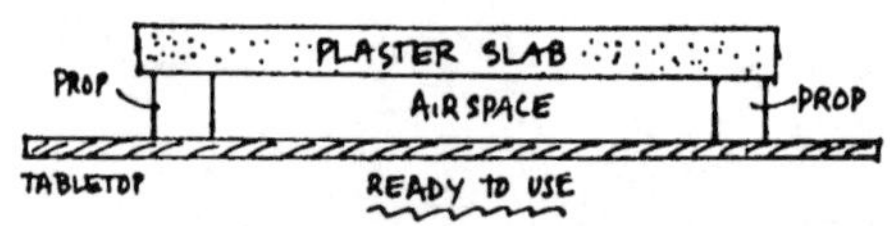

Where to Find Supplies:

These manufacturers can tell you where/who your nearest distributor is for P'Slip® and P'Clay®. Ready to use pugged paper clays can be high fire, low fire, mid-range, earthenware, terracotta and more.

Tuckers Pottery Supply
Richmond Hill (Toronto) Canada

800-304-6185 (toll free)

tel.: 905-889-7705

www.tuckerspottery.com

Distributors include:

Baileys- Kingston NY **800 431-6067 (toll free)** www.baileyspottery.com

Ceramic Supply of New York and New Jersey Lodi. NJ: **800-723-7264 (toll free)** www.7ceramic.com

Clay Art Center
Tacoma,WA

800-952-8030 (toll free)

www.clayartcenter.com

Distributors include: Georgies, Portland OR, Archie Bray, Helena, Montana, Canada, Hawaii, Alaska , Greenbarns (Vancouver, BC)

East Bay Clay Custom Batch
Richmond, CA (San Francisco Bay Area)
510-233-1800 attention: Mike Haney

Industrial Minerals IMCO
Sacramento, CA 916-383-2811

www.clayimco.com

Distributors include:

statewide include Aardvark- southern California and Leslie Ceramics-Berkeley and north.
www.leslie ceramics.com

Mile Hi Ceramics
Denver, Colorado

800-456-0163 (toll free)

www. milehiceramics.com

distributors Montana and Western and Midwestern State

Axner Pottery Supply
Oviedo-Orlando, FL

800-843-7057 (toll free)

www.axner.com

or 407-365-2600- also serves Mexico

Also

www.paperclayart.com may include more source updates.

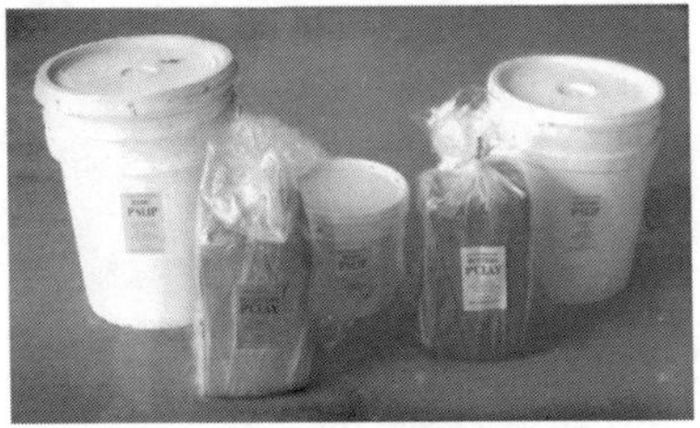

Four Standard Blends of P'Clay® based on vendors existing clay/glaze recipes. (left to right). ***Basic P'Slip®*** *(5 gal.),* ***Sculptor's Blend P'Clay®*** *(25lb. bag, moist.),* ***Basic P'Slip®*** *(1 gal.)* ***Potter's Blend P'Clay®*** *(25lb. bag, moist.),* ***Casting Blend P'Slip®*** *(to pour in plaster molds.)*

Further Study:

Pre-1997 Selected Publications in English by your author.

"Amazing Paper Clay,"
Ceramics Monthly, June 1992.

"Second Generation Ceramics: Technical and Aesthetic Potential of Paper Clay," Interaction in Ceramics, Art, Design, Research, UIAH, Helsinki, Finland 1993. Lecture to the conference: June 1992.

"Paper Clay for Ceramic Sculptors," NCECA Journal (National Council on Education for the Ceramic Arts) Vol. 14. 1993-94, p.14-17. Highlights of 1993 lecture demonstration at San Diego conference.

Paper Clay for Ceramic Sculptors- A Studio Companion First Edition June 1993 Clear Light, Seattle. and New Zealand. Revision 2 1995. This book in your hand is the 3.0. 8 revision, 2008 (Reprint with edited text).

"The Potential of Paper Clay,"
Ceramics, Art and Perception,
(Sidney, Australia) Issue 18, Dec. 1994.

"Magic of Paper Clay," from "Playing with Fire," Symposium and Lecture at Victoria and Albert Museum, London, England. Nov. 1995. *Ceramic Review* (London, UK) Issue 155. Sept.1995.

"Art with Paper Clay, A Global Overview" in Scott, Paul, ed., *"Six Stories From the Paper Clay Revolution,"* Artist Newsletter, London, England, UK, Jan. 1996.

"Paper Clay Ceramics, Recent Artistic and Technical Developments," in Networks in Ceramics, International Conference, June 1996, Edited by Verajankorva and Ahonen, Published by University of Industrial Arts, Helsinki, Finland. 1997. Lecture and Master Class.

"Rules, Rules What Rules with Paper Clay?"
Ceramics Monthly, June 1996.

"Hula Hoops, Ceramic Trash and John Cage... an Artists View from the USA" in "Hot off the Press" (1996), London and UK traveling exhibition catalog ed. by Paul Scott (1996), essay on the influence of "media" on artistic and academic ceramics from the USA, an artist's view.

Books and research more recent include
Jeoung-Ah, Kim (Sweden) Paper-Composite Porcelain, 2006
Gault (in German) Paperclay, Ein Neues Material. Haupt, Verlag Bern, Stuttgart, Wien 1999, 2002, 2006

Early Articles Directly Translated:
Revista Ceramica (Madrid, Spain) in Spanish, 1994 editor translated Spanish.
Gabi Dewald, translator to German: *Keramik Magazin*, (Germany) 1996. Two articles, two issues.

Selected earlier journal article (vol:pp) in addition to op. cit.

Ceramics Technical-Australia,
3:22-8: constructions; 7:36-8 paper clay dragon; 10:75-8 paperclay tiles; 12:67-71 paperclay terra siggilata porcelain; 13:3-7; 13:74-7; 13:78-80 paper slip.
Ceramic Art and Perception-Australia, Gaye Stevens Porcelain imprint paperclay embossed images (see photo page 135). Pottery in Australia-Australia, March 2003- Kay Aldibrand Article (examples of the "chickenwire" school- ed): see also 40:3; 41:4, Steve Harrison "banners of paperclay" fiberglass and pulp.; Campbell-Allen "Where there's smoke, paperclay in anagama" 36 (1)16-18, Gartside articles 33:4; School project: Storytelling and Paper Clay 40:3 70-72.
Ceramic Review-UK,
CR156 Anne Lightwood; CR189- Flexography-photo transfer imprint on paper clay by Helen Smith. also articles by Brian Gartside reprinted from **New Zealand Potter 1994.**
Ceramics Monthly-US,
Linda Mau- *Paper Clay on Steel Mesh*- May 1997;

Lowell Baker, *Spraying Paper Clay,* Nov 1998; Candy Resnick Cover Article: "*Living Tile*" Nov 1995.
Spencer-Cooke, *Porcelain* Dec. 1996.
See also science scholarship by Jeoung, Ah-Kim (Phd Sweden); Srinivisan, et. al. (Australia), and Juvonenen, PhD (Finland)

A Few Ceramic Textbooks:
Gault quoted at length in Robin Hopper ed. Daniel Rhodes "**Clay and Glazes for the Potter**" 2000. Mention of paper clay in many textbooks among them Richard Burkett/Glenn Nelson, Susan Peterson, Paul Scott **Ceramics and Print**.

Early Lecture and Demonstrations:
1991 University of Massachusetts, Amherst; 1992 UIAH University of Industrial Arts and Design, Helsinki Finland, 1993 NCECA, Oregon College of Art and Craft (faculty1993-1994) Los Angeles Chapter of the Design Division of American Ceramic Society 1994; New Zealand, Australia, Clay Today and Royal Academy of Art, Copenhagen, Denmark; and Skaelskor, Victoria and Albert (Playing with Fire), London: UK; Landshut State Ceramic Institute, Germany; 1996 UIAH Helsinki, Finland, Bechyne Symposium Czech Republic; Harvard; University of Delaware; Emily Carr School of Art, Vancouver, BC; plus many summer schools and clay groups.

A Worldwide Grapevine

A wave of controversy over paperclay entered the grapevine in the early 1990's thanks to artists who saw potential and undertook the challenge of paperclay using methods that would have failed in traditional clay that I suggested. I first enjoyed artistic freedom by unorthodox work methods for several years with my recipes in 1990 but it took time for me to sort through the facts of the discovery described on page 8. By 1992, I was moved to report my results and hypothesis. If others were to enjoy benefit of this eco-friendly problem solving medium, I would have to argue the case for its value, and, to call for serious help in field research. At my talk were Kingery, Kim, Juvonen, Hole, and more. Also, I showed works by artists of fired paperclay created by traditional methods together with examples of my paperclay art created by new methods.
Artists and grad students then had the missing pieces of information needed to succeed in "wet on dry." As a result, whether they had previously working with a traditional type of paperclay or not, some put the understanding right into service. Also, thankfully, David Kingery, a prominent scientist, contributed formal material analysis of my samples of paperclay. I was, therefore, delighted to publicize these artists work as part of my demonstration and lecture the following year to the ceramics conference NCECA San Diego March 1993. A thorough patent search was well underway.
To respond to demand for technical help after NCECA, I put together the first spiral bound version of this handbook. Brian Gartside, en route to speak at a conference in Wales (UK), stopped in my studio in Seattle to prepare. He told me he planned to "take the risk of his career" and introduce paperclay as he had witnessed my NCECA demonstration. I created the big dried flat paperclay he used that day. Now even more artists got involved as I had hoped. At my request, Gartside added his articles to mine. The next year, 1994, I demonstrated to hundreds of artists with clays and paper adaptations in 8 countries in 3 continents and sometimes I teamed up with Gartside for this. Soon, established artists adopted part, or all, of the ideas as part of their workshops and teaching. In those years, anyone who had the courage to teach the "wet on dry" was especially needed. Persistent students often had to convince their "old school" professors of it's value too. After a sufficient number of "trials by kiln fire" satisfied skeptics, mention in part, or whole, appeared in the textbooks. Today at many aspects of paperclay are just part of the scene.
When I had been a M.F.A. student in ceramics the 1970's,any fiber could be used to help green strength, but nylon had been preferred over paper pulp. The typical cures for clay involved slowing or stopping shrinkage. Within the context of accepted technical limits, some artists in every continent were showing work of fired paperclay ceramic. In the 1970's, the Japanese sold individually wrapped ready made pliant wet paper thin sheets of paperclay that could be kiln fired that I tried. In France in 1980's methods with porcelain paperclay (Beranger) became known too. The paperclay family also can trace lineage from a long history of sculptures and dwellings made from "not for fire" fiber-clay mixtures that include adobe and the clay fiber mix used today in Kumartuli India.
Many important contributions in front of and behind the scenes such as, but not limited to: SEM micrograph imaging, wood pulp manufacture, and copy centers, set the stage for my piece in the overall puzzle to fit. The "knowledge" expanded to a field of study with plenty of directions still open to explore.

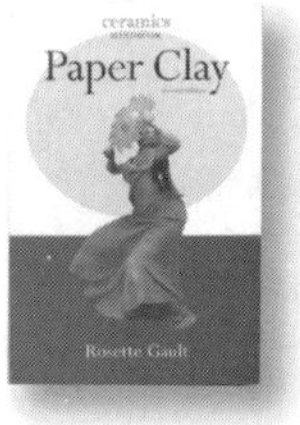

Paper Clay

by Rosette Gault

Full color, features selections of works from artists worldwide as well as information on surface treatments, paper clay bodies, screen print and photo on paper clays, armatures, kilns and more.

Second Edition 2005 USD $26.50

Published by A and C Black, London UK
ISBN 0-7136-6827-X

University of Pennsylvania Press
ISBN 978-0-8122-1895-4 (paperback) in Australia by Artisan Craft Press (Hardcover).

Translations to German ISBN 978-3-258-07125-1 by Alan Haupt Publisher, Switzerland.

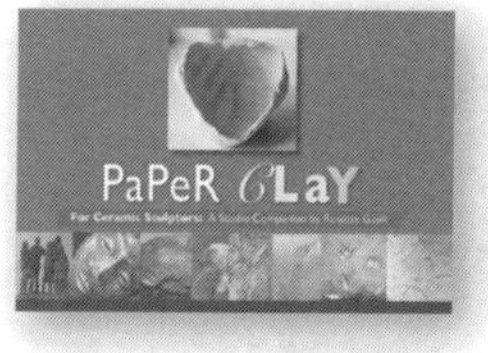

Paper Clay For Ceramic Sculptors Third Edition (v. 3.0.8)

Third edition doubles the size of the original handbook of 1993. Re-edited for version 3.0. 8. Contains over a hundred photos and drawings.

Fourth Printing 2008.

New Century Arts Inc. Seattle
ISBN 978-0-9638793-7-0 (paper)
144 pp paper, b&w USD $22.00

E-Book: For on line reading, order@bookmasters.com
ISBN 978-0-9638793-7-0 (e-book) Order from your local clay supplier, bookstore, or **toll free 24/7 call order line 1 800 247 6553.** Major Credit Cards Accepted. $22 plus $4.00 Shipping/Handling USD or overseas $22.00 plus $8.00 Shipping/Handling USD. Or send pre-payment and shipping address to PaperClay 3.8 ; PO Box 388; Ashland, Ohio 44805 Wholesale discount to trade: minimum order of 6: FAX 419-281-6883. (add Ohio Residents sales tax 6.5% or Washington State Residents 8.9%)

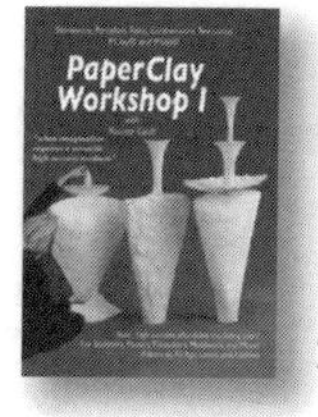

DVD

PaperClay Workshop I

with Rosette Gault

2 hours.

Over 16 demonstration segments of video plus slide show extras.

See handbuilding, figurative or abstract form, coil, pinch, slab, bas relief, alterations to bone dry, assembly, slabcraft, modeling, potters wheel throwing, pulp preparation and mixing, speed wedging and more.

Extras: Four extra slide shows include "Beginner Basics Lessons" in pinch, coil and slab hand building and "Potters Wheel"

DVD 06 Edition 1.0.0

ISBN 0-9638793-2-4

ISBN 13: 978-0-9638793-2-5

$39.95

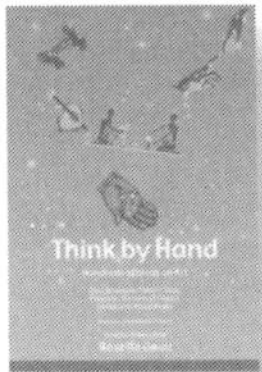

Think By Hand

A catalog of 496 "seed" visual trigger images and project possibilities for makers from antiquity to present day, and beyond.

The ideas range from simple to sophisticated. All are suitable for execution in all variety of traditional art media as well as the versatile P'Clay.

Teachers may save time in lesson plans and assignments. This is the art school brief in a single book I as a teacher always wanted when planning my classes.

ISBN 973-0-9638793-1-8 or 9638793-1-6

$24.00 US

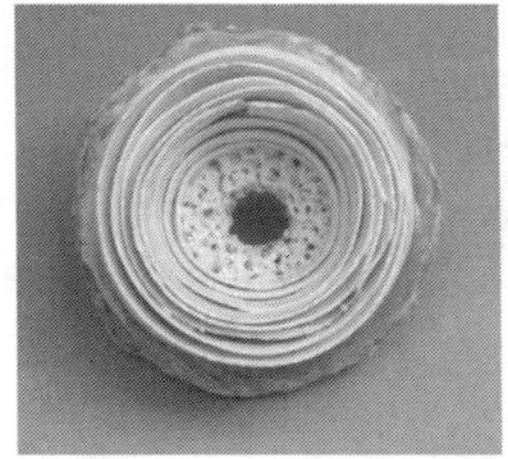

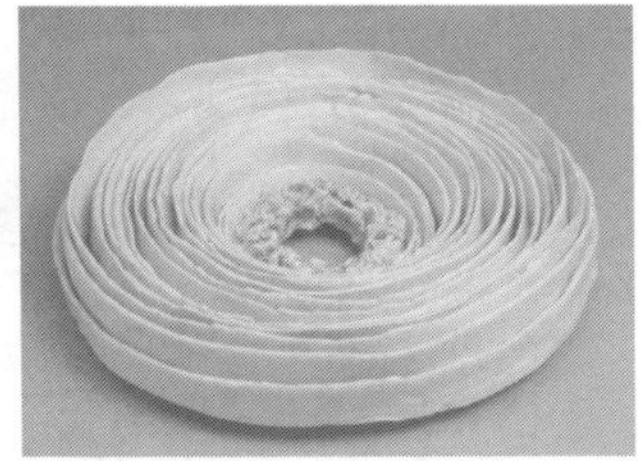

"Close to a Bone" Series
porcelain paperclay works by author each diameter 6- 8"

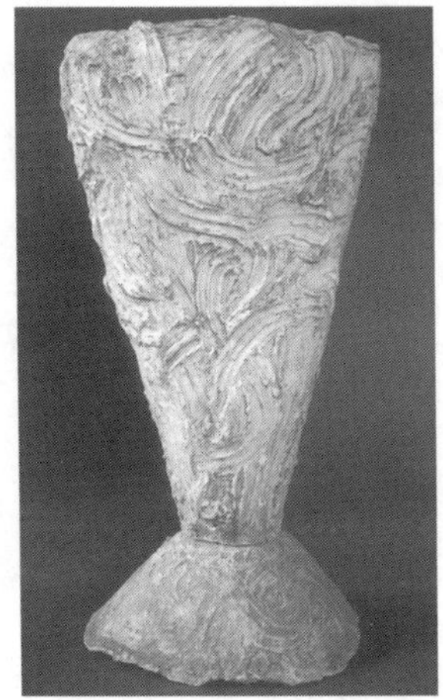

"Deaf-Mute"
by author
Paste of P'Slip was applied as a "thick" smear over bone dry assembled shell forms.
Eathenware cone 4, 48" ht.

Research Ideas

Use for Prototypes and Models

Since soft paperclay can be modeled, and dried paperclay as a hard surface can be altered and repaired indefinitely, more types of revisions are in the repertoire. For example, Randy Wood worked out designs for screw blades within rotary vacuum pug mills machines. Ceramic design students in Copenhagen's Royal Academy choose paper clay to master complex multiple nesting dinnerware service designs.

Photos below: Prototypes for a "close fitting nested parts" assignment at Design School in Copenhagen, Denmark. (Students of M. Thorsen.) Bone dried parts can be handled and altered.

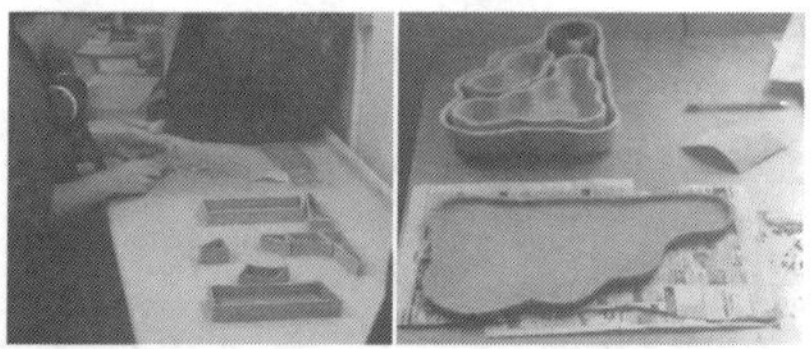

Recycle of Industrial Waste

Jon Williams and I, with the support of Sonoma Tile in California, in the mid 1990's collaborated and conducted research on the feasibility of paper clays in ram press and various blends of recycled scrap glaze with a variety of recycled plain and ultra ink-loaded pulps. Jon created earthenware paper clay tiles made from "recycled everything scrap" that test less than one percent in porosity after fire.

Water Filtration

The pores in ceramic filters from sawdust, rice, et. alia, are *too big* to physically trap bacteria. So, after the firing, all of these need soaking in a bath of disinfectant, such as silver nitrate. It's likely that voids of "tip ends" of cellulose fiber could be aligned and compressed in a certain way to be delicate enough to do the job on their own. (See detail on pages 80-81 and Chapter 5.) With a paperclay water filtration system, each filter could come out of the kiln fire sanitized and ready to use. After voids clog, exchange the filter for a cleaned one, like a bottle is recycled.

Models on right for water filters by author. Submerge kitchen friendly hand sized filter in a bucket of unclean water. Use a foot pedal vacuum pump to suck water in through the bottom and side of the filter walls. Drinking straws show how cleaned water would exit through a hose to fill cups, etc. The manufacture can be more efficient because cast and /or extruded parts are assembled bone dried.

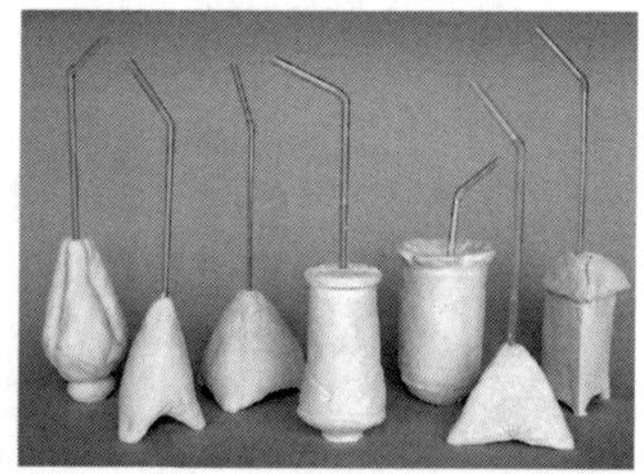

I had a hunch that a viable ceramic paperclay filter could be made efficiently, even in a "low tech" village situation. It was confirmed in 2006. I teamed up with Jon Williams and Ron Rivera of Potters for Peace to create paperclay fired water filters in a Nicaraguan village factory using only recycled Managua City newsprint and local terra cotta clay. Initial tests for flow rate were conducted successfully. The process could be adapted almost anywhere in the world. Detailed research is needed.

The cost of domestic filtration to the average family in many developing countries, particularly in the rural areas is still beyond reach. Locally managed manufacture, distribution, and small business service networks are not near what they could be. The development of an efficient production technology ideally ought be funded in such a way that democratic access to the technical results fosters a network of local fair trade for the service. Diplomats, linguists, and teachers will also be needed.

Access to clean drinking water and filtration is a human right that not just rich people deserve. Please join the effort to *end this world health problem* as soon as possible.

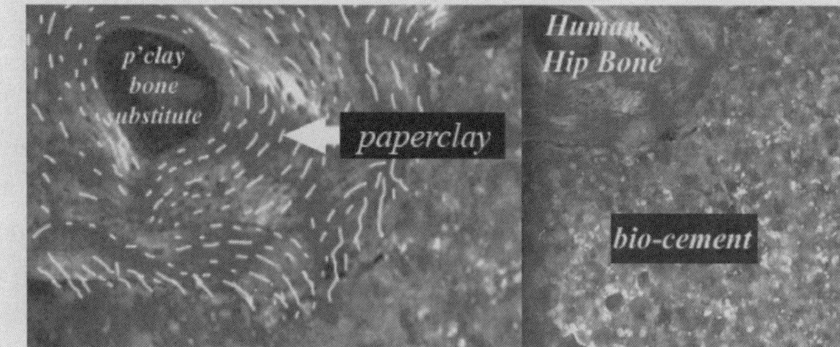

Artist Vision: Custom Human Bone Prosthesis

In the set of cross section micrographs above, to right is a human bone with a bio-cement that has "adhesion problems." Adhesion, long term, is also an issue with a metal prosthesis. To left is a close up of the same micrograph with an overlay sketch of white lines to suggest how cellulose pores might show on a micrograph had the prosthesis had been made in part of paperclay ceramic. The bio-cement could then seep a bit into the pores of the prosthesis for a better grip. *To create a prosthesis bone,* the process will involve aligning cellulose fiber in successive layers over top of a pre-cast hollow form of the "bubble porous" form of ceramic (detail is available). The manufacture method simulates the natural growth patterns in human bone with precision variations in density, composition, structure, contour along the way. In addition, the base ceramic material would mimic composition of human bone.

For weight bearing ball and socket joints, points of bone contact need be a very hard polished smooth paperclay surface. The alignment, orientation and density of clay particles for this special purpose in paperclay can be adapted for this.

Research is needed.
Paperclay might be tested also for application in heat shields because it can "flex" in thermal shock, function as a refractory for heat insulation and is light weight in a different way than traditional clay.
Fire rock hard zirconium ceramic base clay and hardwood pulp together and observe how the colloidal minerals from the cellulose ash seals the interior of each pore. Collaborative research between ceramic engineers, materials scientists, and biotechnology specialists will soon be more common than it used to be.

Rethink Water Based Manufacture
High compression dry clay powder press systems solves many of the issues (like less waste from breakage) that paper clay water based industrial technology also solves If eco-friendly paperclay technology is used, it will work in the older water based equipment and is affordable. Spray glaze application over greenware for single fire is feasible. Durable greenware can be moved ,pre easily. Certain blends of P'Clay prove well in existing ram press equipment.

Industrial Air or Fluid Intake or Exit "Scrubbers"
Filters of paperclay can trap fluid hot airborne particles. This too could be tested.

Building Material and Sanitary Ware
Cast parts would be less vulnerable to loss in transit before firing. If breakage did happen, repair or replacement can occur of just the damaged part not the whole thing. Water based manufacture could continue. Shipping fees could be less if the finish weight is less. Whether these advantages balance the cost of the added cellulose could be studied.
Paperclay is a refined form of "high-tech adobe" and some success and stability with paper clays has been reported.
Also, as mentioned, so called "old fashioned" forming equipment can be adapted to handle water based paperclay.

Art Materials of the Future

Product 1. Ready to carve "chunks" of paperclay. I see kits of near solid sintered porcelain P'Clay cube, egg, and cylinder shapes to carve on, complete with a fettle tool and a little sponge to wipe up carving dust.
Product 2. Air dried cast slabs sheets of 12"x12"x 3/4" plain bone dry P'Clay These are ready to saw on, build with, use for tile, or store and slake down in water for making P'Clay as desired in the studio. Unlike pugged soft P'Clay®, these sheets of dry P'Clay® have no limit on shelf life. Plus measuring is easy and water weight nil.

More Thanks to:

Research for this big project was sponsored in part by a series of residency grants over many years from the Banff Centre for the Arts in Alberta Canada.

So many people helped from behind and in front of the scenes to offer thoughts and reports, to discuss the idea, and to have courage to try it. Your ongoing inquiries kept me thinking and working on this over the what has turned out to be years of work. I am eternally thankful and I trust emerging generations of artists and sculptors will be too. Rosemary, Ed, Les, Linda, Paul, Glenys, Garry, Robin, Trudy, Joe, Zak, Howard, Erik, Diane, Brian, Frank, Nina, Priscilla, Susan, Ryan, Paul, Jindra, Elzbieta, Carol, Linda, Rhonda, Kathy, Steph, David, Ken, John, Carol, Carolyn, Matthew, Gale, Nancy, Betsy, Louise, Mike, John, Ken, Teresa, Robin, Jean-Paul and Abe, Laura, and many others who have contributed to the success of this project. Helpful proof commentary and suggestions from Janet Mansfield, Ruth Butler, Gale Macleod Colby Mirzayanov, and Masguda Shamsutinova and others were invaluable. Please accept my apology if I omitted you or someone important, in this, or my other book. Please tell me, so I can correct this in the future. I thank my teachers for patience with me over the years. Encouragement from senior colleagues, Jean Griffith, Toshiko Takaezu, Peter Voulkos, Rudy Autio, Jim Melchert, Lamar Harrington, Betty Woodman, Howard Kottler, Victor Spinski, Shojo Imoto (an inventor of an early form of paperclay circa 1970's), and many other seniors was invaluable. Far sighted Tapio Yli Vikari and his staff, of UIAH in Finland. Nancy La Pointe tested the first batches of low fire terra cotta with me for wet on dry etc. at a workshop at the University of Massachusetts in 1991.

"Book" by Tui Nhah

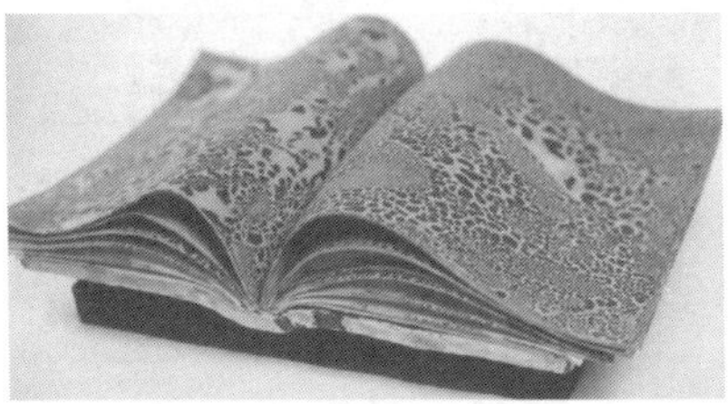

I thank all those who sponsored thea early demonstration lectures. Because of you, paperclay spread as fast as it did nearly 20 years ago. Today, more teachers pass it forward for generations of artists to come. I was honored to serve everyone involved.

In order to have time to research and write this revision, still more people have been involved with financial and emotional support.

right: Forty Below (-40C) in a Canada winter test for two years. Glazed paperclay pure porcelain ceramic work by author.

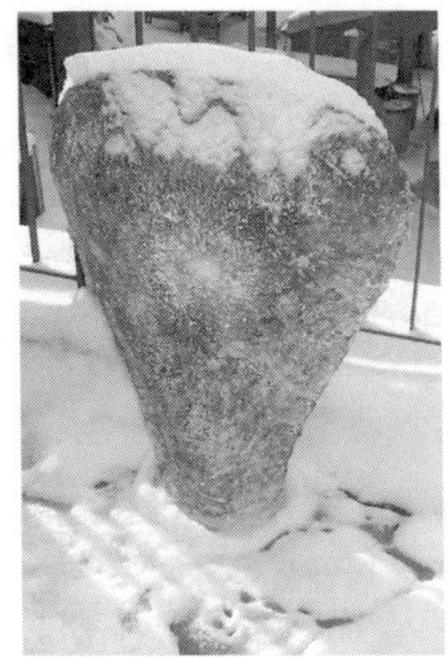

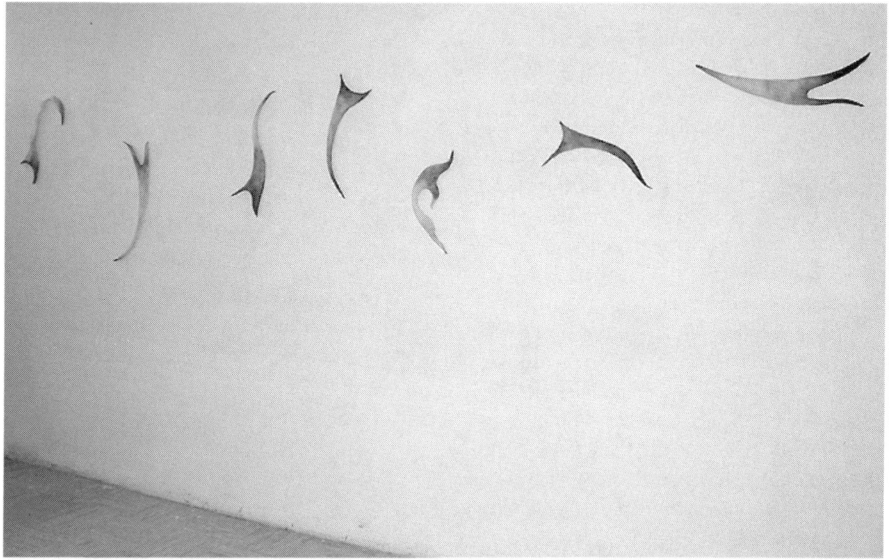

"Dance Bones"
Collection for Wall
Smoked and Flamed High-fired
Porcelain Paperclay by Rosette Gault,
USA

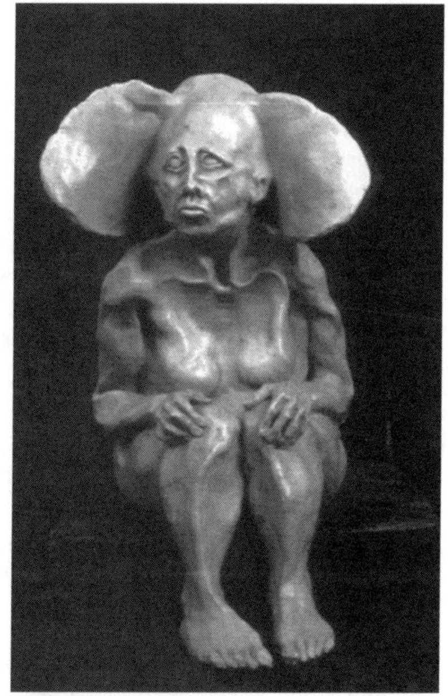

Seated Figure
by Kathy Ross
USA

More Art "Experiments"

1. ***Drum*** by Ann Sanders. Earthenware. Made by means of dry coils stacked up per the illustration on page 22. Wet leather skin was stretched over rim and dried tight.

2. "***Fun Form"*** by Author. From firing (and sometimes over firing) shapes like these, I came to understand the logical patterns that inform paperclay movement inside the kiln. I came to understand reinforcement also.

3. The ***"Dip Trip"*** Dip organic items, twigs, and etc. in P'Slip, let them dry. Dip as many times as you want to thicken the coating layers. Lose natural surface detail, but keep basic shape. Fire only in well ventilated kiln. Garry Williams "rabbit" branches on the cover of my second book **Paper Clay** (photo on p.121) were dipped and fired to biscuit, before he joined them to his, at the time unfired, clay rabbit.

4. "***The Pot Family Balance***" work in progress by author, all P'Clay. In the early days I tested the idea that bone dry could join with P'Slip and not crack, at every opportunity.

5. ***Tile Project*** by Carol Gaskin and Peter Berry (6 x 8 feet). Pour a giant low pool of fresh made high pulp P'Slip into wood frame set on plasterboard. The wood frame was removed and the tiles air dried flat.

1.

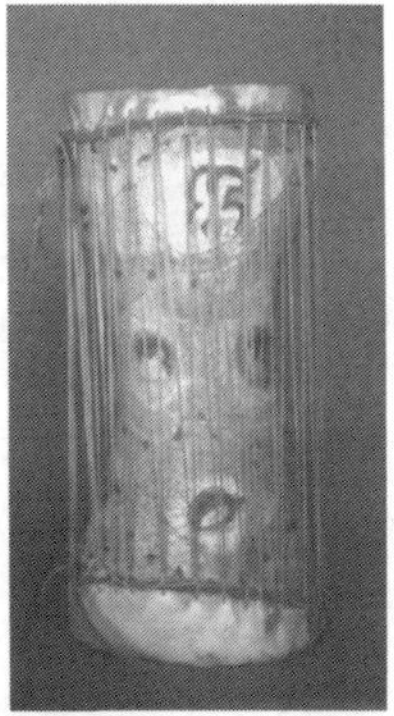

2.

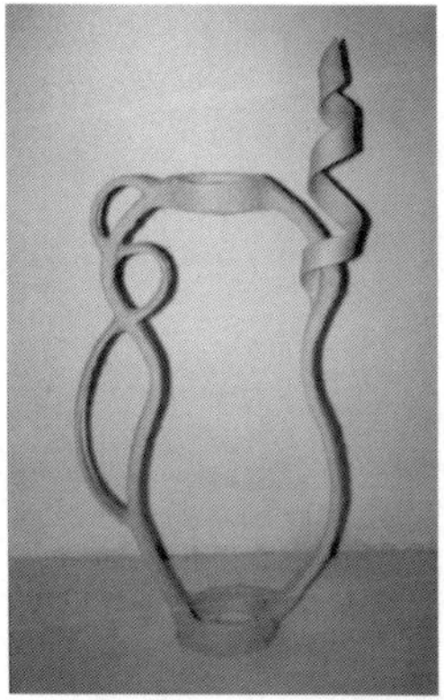

3.

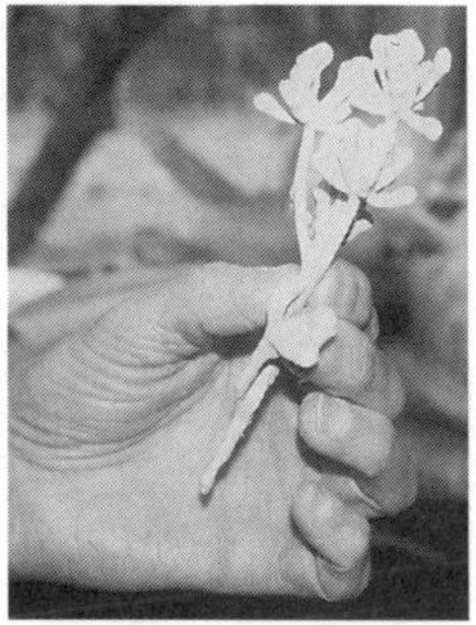

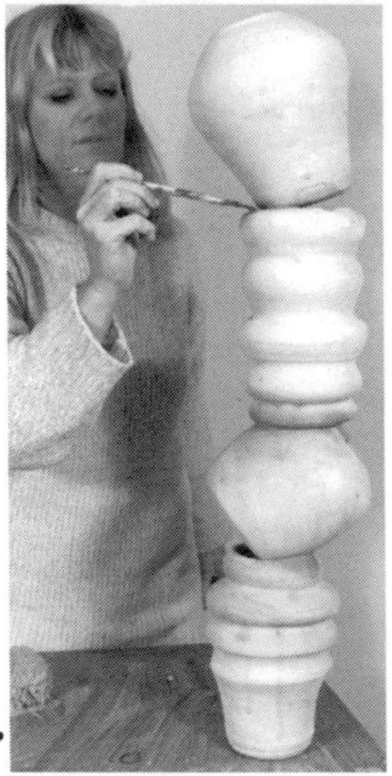

4.

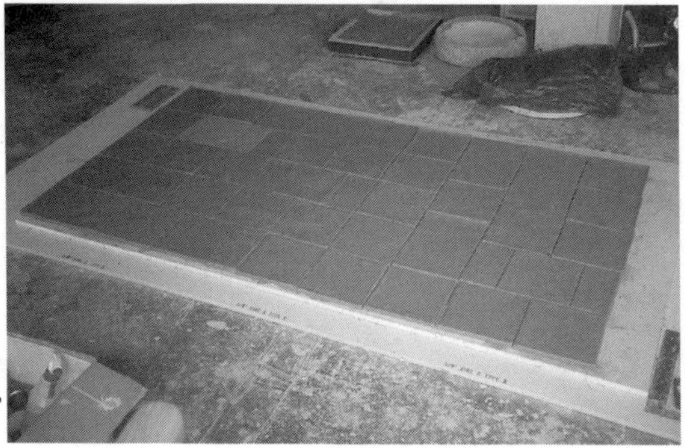

5.

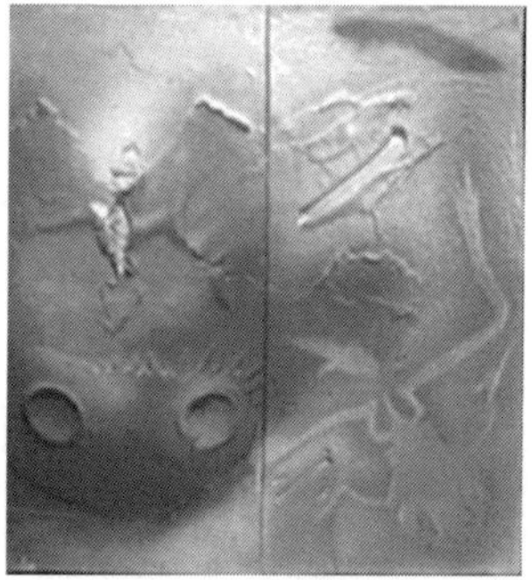

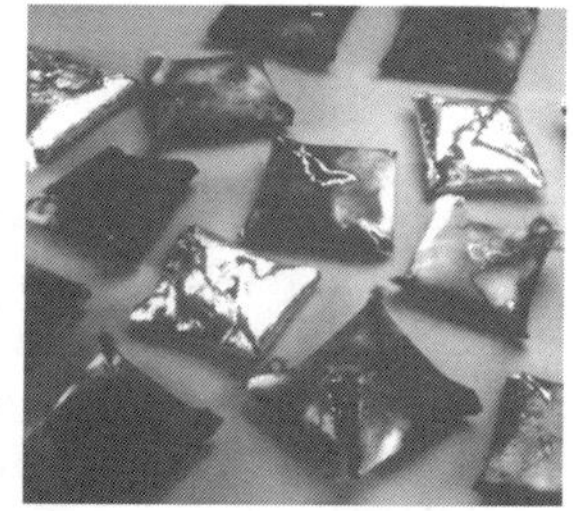

"Dream Boxes"
Diane Baxter USA.
Super thin folded, pit fire, and gold leaf. Each is sized to fit in palm of hand.

"Detail of Frog Theme Mural and Tryptych"
Carol Gaskin and Peter Berry
Seamless "blend" between leather soft stretched slab into and over ultra large flat bone tiles and Note integration between surface with surface relief and contour. Bas-relief in clay will never be be the same.

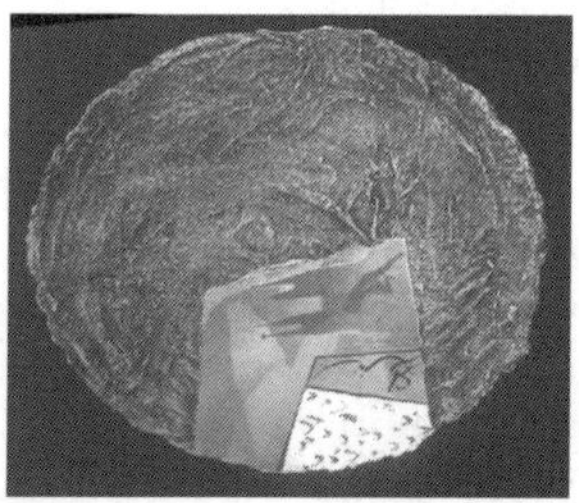

"Disk"
Ed Bamiling
Canada

Raku fired Oval Wall Plate
12 x 15 inches or so.

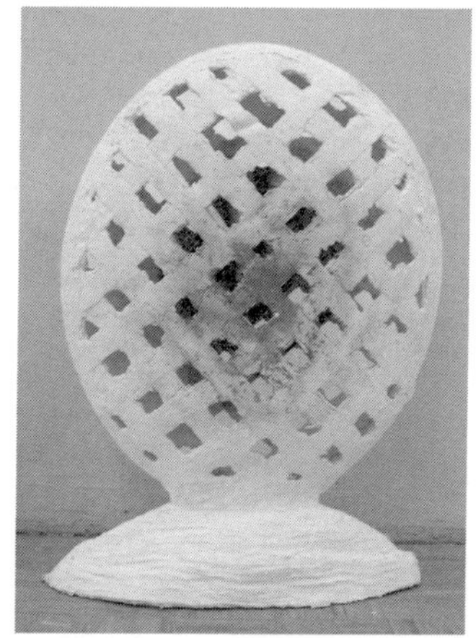

"Trap"
Porcelain paperclay sculpture 32 in/81cm ht. by Rosette Gault

Glossary

When I was a beginner, a list like this would have helped.

Bisque or Biscuit Fired: an intermediate "halfway done" fire required in traditional pottery to make traditional clay harden enough that it can't dissolve, or lose shape, dipped in water during glaze application. The cone range is stated as cone 08 to cone 02. The average time to fire and cool down is about 20 hours- a whole day.

Chamotte: a fancy word for **grog.**

Clay: microscopic flat chips of ancient mineral deposited by ancient rivers above or below ground. Big deposits are dug up and bagged as dry mineral powders. When the dry powder is mixed with water it is moist and pliant for modeling. Traditional pure clay dries up in crack patterns in the sun. It used to be potters had to use the nearest clay, but nowadays, clays are mixed from distant mines.

Cones: store-bought temperature measuring pointy pyramids of clay calibrated to melt or bend at precise temperatures in kilns. There is approximately 10 degrees of difference between each cone. Each cone has a specific temperature range matches its number. The identifying numbers go up in order from the lowest heat of a cone 032 for the most delicate china paints, and gold and silver lustres, pass through bisque cones: O8, 05, 04, and on up through mid range cones: 1, 2, 3, 4, and through to high fire cones: 8, 9, 10, 11, 12 and hotter still: up to cone 31 or so. Many ceramic textbooks will have lists of specifics. During fire the potter opens peep holes and looks in to see how many of certain numbered cones have melted down yet. The decision to cut the fuel off and end the fire on a kiln is usually determined by this.

Engobe: a type of slip.

Fire: see bisque.

Glaze: can be matte to gloss after the fire. The coating goes on wet in a liquid- but melts into glass coating during the fire. Many colors and choices of this exist. Glaze is powdered glass stirred up to suspension in water. When the potter dips a dry water absorbent bisque or dry absorbent paper clay in a bucket of liquid glaze, the water soaks into the open matte pores of the pot, and soon evaporates. What's leftover is a perfect even coating of the powder! But the powder is very vulnerable to fingerprints as these disturb the uniform surface deposit.

Grog: ground up bisqued clay bricks. The granulation varies from fine to coarse. It is inert at low temperatures and slightly water absorbent.

High Fire: glaze would melt to gloss around 1250C (cone 8-10.)

Low Fire: glaze would melted to gloss around 1000C (cone 04)

Oxidation: kiln atmosphere is a condition of red hot "air" that is burning clean- it has just amount of fuel it needs to stay hot.

Paperclay: trademarked name for a white "hobby clay" that is a refined plasticised papier-maché used mostly for dolls heads, jewelers, and the like. Would not survive ceramic firing. See page 61.

P'Clay: traditional clay with a lesser percentage of pulp uniformly dispersed in the mixture.

P'Slip: watered down form of P'Clay.

Porcelain: a white pure clay that can be translucent like glass when thin and high fired to about 1250C.

Reduction: describes a hot kiln atmosphere with more fuel present to burn than fire really needed. Thus, lefotver hot gas turns to dark pungent smoke. Melting glazes and clays in the kiln change colors during this time period.

Slip: watered down clay, usually fires to matte finish.

Stoneware: a high fire clay that is not white, that holds water.

Terra Siggilata: a super refined form of slip that buffs to a satin matte patina final finish.

Underglaze: a clay slip that has some colored stain or oxide in it. It fires matte, so glazes will melt well on top of it.

Vitrify: to turn to glass, to melt enough to seal water out.

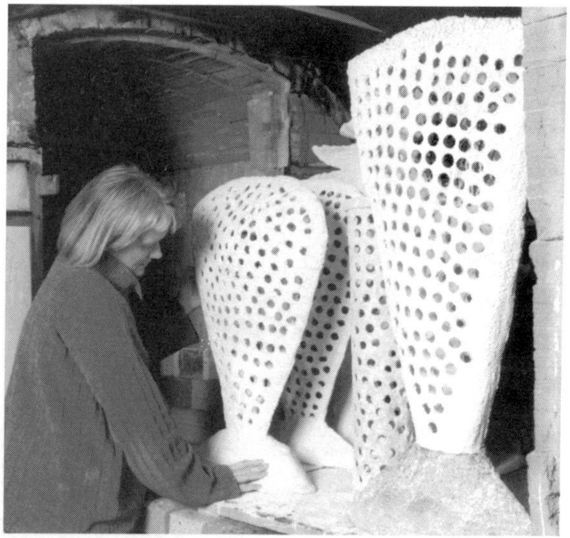

Assembly Strong Enough for Transit
Author loads air dried works in kiln.
Works of low fire cone 04 earthenware based paperclay can be fired hotter than normal.
At cone 4-6 they come out with a hardness and density similar to a white stoneware.

Index

N

O

P

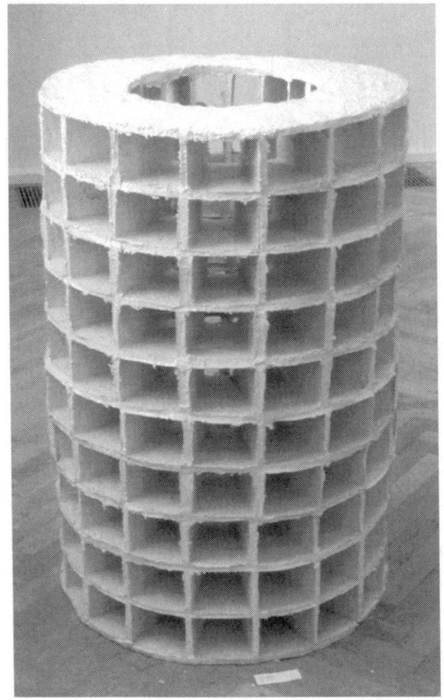

"Strucktur" by Esben Klenman, Denmark

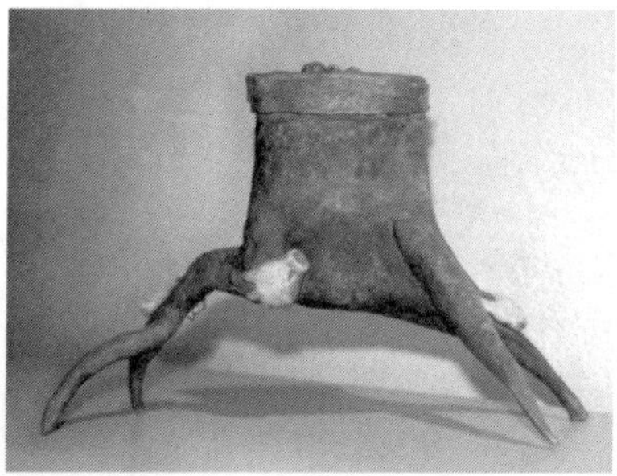

"Restless Tree Trunk with Eggs Journeys Home" by Author about 6" Ht. (1993)

T

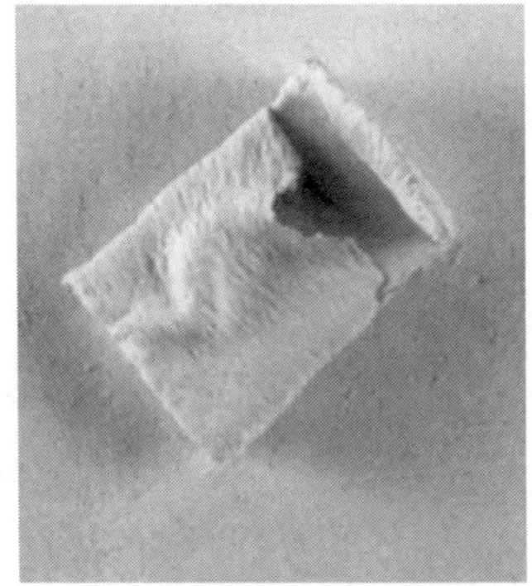

Detail from "Aerial," Wall work by author. 11"x 17" earthenware

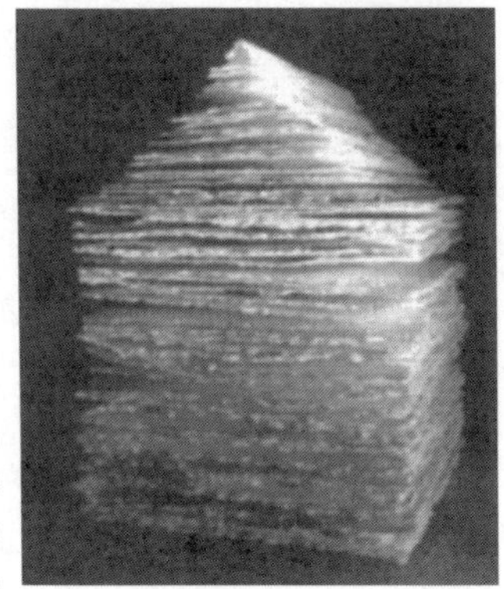

Gaye Stevens, Australia from series of porcelain with watermark thin imprints.

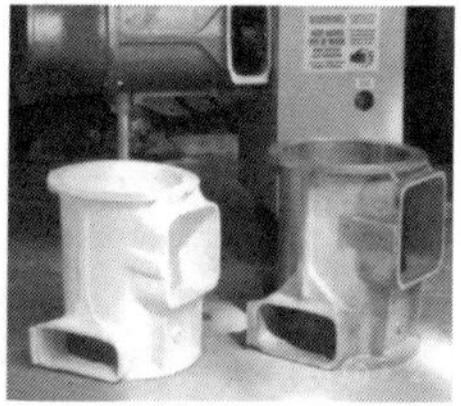

Models for machine parts made in paper clay by Randy Wood at Peter Pugger Manufacturing in California.

Cover Photos
Bowl by Malene Pederson, Denmark,l
l-r: Ann Verdacourt, NZ
all others by/of author, Karen Thrasher photo
Back Cover Photos by:
Author
except Dan Keegan exhibit, Carol Ladas Gaskin and Peter Berry "Pneuvmatos" Mural detail and detail peacock tile bas-relief by Cynthia Dahlstrom

Graphic design, typesetting, layout by author.

Illustrations
Gault 15, 20, 22, 23, 28, 30, 31 33, 34, 42, 47, 51, 52, 57, 58, 77, 78, 84, 85, 86, 87, 89, 91, 99, 101, 103, 107, 109, 110, 114, 115, 116, 125
Clip art 10, 14, 124

Photo credits
Dahlstrom 50, 52
Gaskin, Carol 129, 130
Gault 7, 11, 12, 13, 16, 24, 25, 30, 40, 41, 44, 49, 51, 53, 63, 65, 67, 68, 69, 72, 74, 73, 117, 134, 125, 121, 122, 129, 130, 134, 135
Hungerford, Susan 25, 26, 27, 29, 31
Hvasbo 64
Keller 81
Kingery 82, 82
Klenman 133
Lang 64
Lee, Don 132
Malcahy 36
Micrograph 81 Walter Keller courtesy of *Scientific American* 1978
Micrographs 77, 78, 79, 80 courtesy Paulette Long, ed. **Paper Art and Technology** World Print Council San Francisco 1979 by way of Institute of Paper Chemistry, Appleton Wisconsin 1974
papers in light page 76 credited to S. Rowan (**Recycled Papers the Essential Guide** by C. Thompson 1992)
Simms, Bev 38
Slocum, Ree, 74
Thrasher, Karen, Cover
Verdacourt 136
Wood, Randy, 127

Works in process
Dahlstrom 50, 52
Gaskin and Berry 129
Gault 24, 25, 27, 31, 38, 39, 40, 41, 42, 44, 63, 65, 67, 68C, 69, 74, 123,
Thorsen, M 124

Art Works Documentation
Bamiling 130
Baxter,130
Gault 7, 11, 12, 16, 40, 49, 53 (finished, ready to install) 72, 73, 130, 134, 135, 136, 140
Gaskin and Berry, Cover, 130
Hvasbo 64
Keegan: cover
Klenman 133
Lang 64
Mulcahy 36
Nhah, Tui 127
Ross 128
Stevens 137
Verdacourt 139, cover

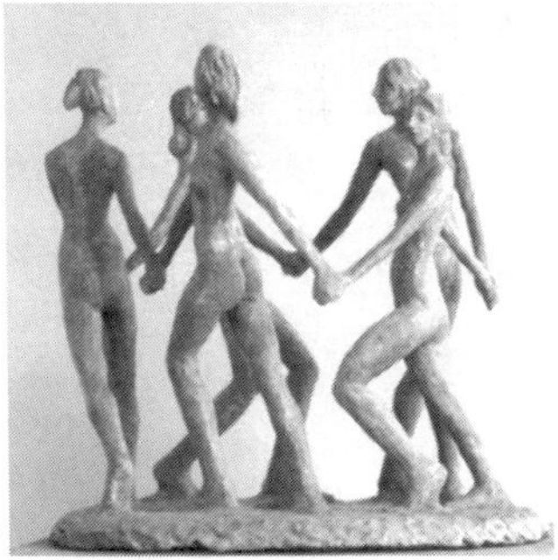

Figures by Ann Verdacourt, New Zealand

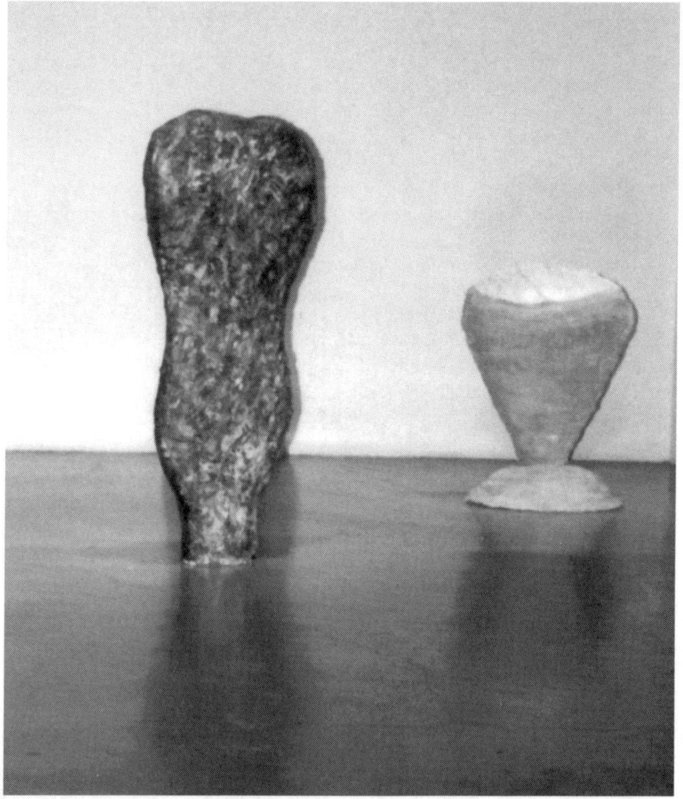

Elementals

"Trap for Dark Matter and Shadows" (left)

"Compressed Orange with a Theoretical Straw,"

Freestanding by Author.
(taller one stands nearly 4 feet)
Exhibit in Seattle 1999.

Meet Your Author

Rosette Gault was born in New York City. She earned her M.F.A in Ceramics in 1978 at the University of Puget Sound in 1978 and her B.A. in Communication from the University of Colorado at Boulder in 1975. She began her study of pottery with Betty Woodman and Larry Clark in 1971. She has been practicing studio ceramic arts ever since. Listed in "Who's Who in America," holder of a U.S. Patent, she is also author of several books. Her award winning ceramic work has been shown widely since 1978. She has taught at many of the top schools in the world. Find more of her projects on **www.rosettestudio.net.**

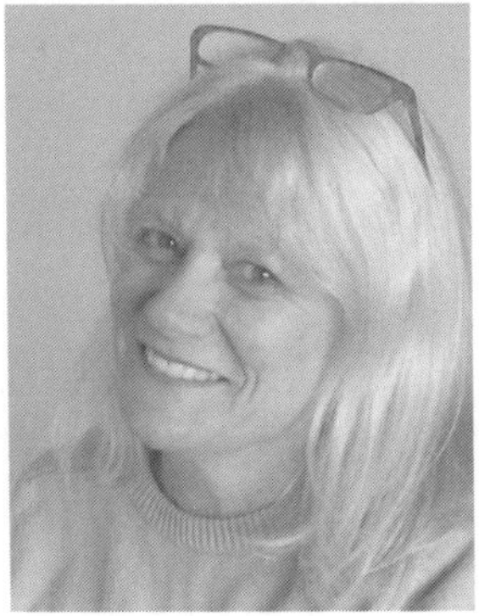

Notes: